RUST BELT FEMME

RUST BELT FEMME

RAECHEL ANNE JOLIE

Belt Publishing

Printed in the United States of America
First Edition
1 2 3 4 5 6 7 8 9

ISBN: 978-1-948742-63-4

Belt Publishing
3143 W. 33rd Street #6
Cleveland, Ohio 44109
www.beltpublishing.com

Book design by Meredith Pangrace
Cover by David Wilson

For Momma,
for Northeast Ohio,
and for working class femmes.

"To be femme is to give honor where there has been shame."
—Mykel Johnson

"Identity ... has always been central to working-class movements."
—Robin D. G. Kelley

This book about my deep love of the soil and sky that comprises Northeast Ohio is actually a book about my deep love of the soil and sky that comprises stolen Iroquois land. I am indebted to the work of indigenous activists and healers who have taught me to remember this and name it as often as I can, and more than that, to find ways to reduce the harm of the presence of white colonizers on this land. During the writing of this book, I began making monthly donations to the Committee of 500 Years of Dignity and Resistance, a grassroots 501(c)(3) in Cleveland dedicated to maintaining indigenous culture and heritage.

"The real truth about it is
My kind of life's no better off
If I've got the maps or if I'm lost."

—Songs: Ohia

Prologue

Our first home was a modest ranch house on Tinkers Creek Road, tucked in between the quiet, rural street and the "crick," where we'd go to skip rocks and hunt for treasures. As a young girl, I thought the front yard went on for miles, but when I go back to Ohio as an adult, I see it's just about twenty-five feet of grass. It felt immense though, in its expansiveness, in its ability to act as a landscape for so much joy and so much agony—the place where I caught lightning bugs on summer nights, attempted somersaults next to broken-down cars, chased playfully after our Newfoundland mutt; the place that absorbed the gasoline mixed with blood from my father's skull, that acted as a landing strip for the emergency helicopter, that muffled my mother's screams as she collapsed against the soil upon discovering his mangled body.

But the lightning bugs are what I remember most vividly, which is a gift, given the circumstances. The lightning bugs on Tinkers Creek were actually magic, I think, and maybe it was my first foray into witchcraft when at five years old, I held up my tiny hands and let their iridescent wings flutter against the lines of my palms. They were sacrificed in rituals some nights, too. Once, a boy down the street, David,* who was my first crush, clasped my shut palms with his and asked me to pass him the glowing bug. When he got hold of it, quickly without pause, he ripped the pulsing green bulb from the insect's body. I shrieked in protest, but just as quickly, he fashioned jewelry with a blade of grass, and the still-glowing green became the rock of an engagement ring.

This memory is a frequent one in my mind. I think about the glimmer of the decapitated bug on my ring finger, and when I do, I feel the warm night air on my skin, the coolness of our overgrown grass against my bare feet. I hear the sound of the neighborhood kids who seemed to gather instinctively in any number of front yards, with or without parental supervision, all of us together a sturdy gang of working-class children with dirty feet and wild imaginations. Some of us were safer away from our homes than inside them, and if anyone needed help, we would find it from each other.

Working-class people are very good at taking care of one another because no one else will do it for us. And Mom was, after a certain point, the best at it of anyone because she eventually got sober. Our home was always covered in piles of unfolded laundry and unpaid bills, the cat litter boxes were never clean, and the television was always on, but she wasn't drinking, and that was bigger and more important than anything else. On many days after "the accident," she barely held it together, but her sobriety was the dividing line between getting by and falling apart. And so, it wasn't uncommon for these nights of mischief and adventure to conclude in our living room with Kool-Aid, pizza rolls, and a Blockbuster VHS.

My days look a lot different now, and not just because I'm an adult. I'm what one therapist called a "class-straddler," which I prefer to "class-transitioner," because the truth is, there's never not a foot of mine firmly in Valley View, eating processed food, watching stolen cable, and going to stock car races. A PhD and multiple major-city addresses can never change that being poor is written in my blood and my bones as much as it is sung from my tight skirts and cheap lipstick. Being poor became the building blocks of my gender. This embodied expression we in the queer community call "femme." It's a type of feminity that I have come to realize is inextricable from the shape of early poverty, the shades of the rural edges of Cleveland, and for me, the sound of punk.

In between then and now are Northeast Ohio landmarks that left scars, sometimes like kisses and sometimes like razor blades. I was seduced out of my poor "white trash" town, first into the arms of the artist culture on Coventry Road, then later by the punks in Lakewood. "White trash," a term that is problematic, has become one that I, along with Dorothy Allison, have reclaimed insofar as the "trash" part is concerned—I've grown to find more pride than shame in where I come from. My life between the accident and where I am now is a sepia-tinted montage of Nirvana songs and choker necklaces, lesbian witches and local coffee shops, tight black jeans and band T-shirts, and the billows of charcoal steel mill smoke I'd pass on my way to the record store.

This story, then, is about growing up in poverty in rural Ohio, finding hope in the alternative culture I discovered in Cleveland, and how my complicated love for these people and these places is a tenacious part of everything I've done since leaving it. Every bit of it turned me into the queer femme feminist writer I am today, and no number of degrees or fancy vocabulary words will ever be enough for me to forget that.

I look back on my life with some romance, but poverty is as damaging as it is enriching. I was diagnosed with complex post-traumatic stress disorder (C-PTSD) after an incident on my thirtieth birthday that led me to screaming at the top of my lungs on a frozen street in Montreal. Since confronting the broken parts of me—the impact of unpaid utility bills, the pain of childhood sexual assault, the abandonment issues that come along with losing a father—my brain works a little differently. Trauma has a way of mixing up the beginnings and middles, of never feeling an ending to any of it. This is how things have been for me; time no longer linear, but existing in fragments of presence and remembering, sometimes consecutive, sometimes simultaneous. And so my story is like this. Flashes of my early life sliding against the hindsight that helps you tell the story better.

I am offering this story of a queer midwestern life to you in these pieces and parts, like spirits who materialize in the shadows when they are feeling restless and forgotten. There is no way to make entirely coherent a life that is more assemblage than intersections, an existence that weaves in and out of time and space. But I think you'll be able to follow along, because whether our neurology is burdened by trauma or not, I think most of us who are drawn to memoir are burdened with an incurable case of nostalgia.

I began with the memory of the lightning bug because no matter how far away I get, I see so clearly that chartreuse glow balancing against my knuckle, the persistent remains of the dismembered alchemist, against all odds, living on. And I think that indelible resilience reminds me of home—of Ohio—more than anything.

PART 1

THE ACCIDENT:
VALLEY VIEW, OHIO

1.
Champions of the World

The hot-pink stuffed elephant wore a yellow hat on its head, which was now covered on one side with my vomit. My dad had bought it for me from the circus we attended at the Richfield Coliseum earlier that week. I named him Dumbo, and slept with him every night, usually snuggled between my parents in their bed. Now I was in their bed again, whimpering about the pain in my belly and the smell of my bile. I threw Dumbo off the bed into a pile of clothes. Mom stroked the wispy blonde strands of hair from my face, gently wiped the corners of my mouth, and helped me take sips of water.

I was three years old, almost four, and just a few days prior had been so excited to be in a circus tent. The extravagance of it all was something completely new to me, and it was a big deal that my parents saved up enough money to get us tickets. Getting a stuffed, hot-pink elephant as a memento thrilled me, and I clung to it with delight, the fuzzy pink fur against my tiny fingers a kind of soft reminder that even though we were poor, I was still a kid who went to the circus and whose parents bought her souvenirs.

So it's really no wonder when my dad came in the bedroom to help take care of me, that the first thing he did was look for Dumbo. He spotted it on the floor and picked it up without noticing the streak of vomit on Dumbo's side. "Here you go," he cooed, placing the elephant on the pillow by my face.

"No!" I shrieked, and threw it off the bed.

My dad's face fell. I was so young, I can't imagine that I possibly had a mature enough sense of empathy to have fully understood the implications of the pain that may have caused him, but I do remember, vividly, knowing he was hurt.

"She threw up on it, Mike," my mom explained, but my head was buried back in the pillow and my eyes were closed, so I didn't notice if his face had changed or not.

This is the last memory I have of my father before he was hit by a drunk driver in our front yard. I don't remember how many days or weeks or maybe even months before the accident that this memory actually occurred, but it is the final one I have.

———————

My dad worked second shift in a factory in Cleveland, so he got home late enough to encounter people driving home from the bar. We lived on a rural street in the village of Valley View, a small town of 2,000 people, about twenty-five minutes from the city. One night after work, Daddy took out the garbage, walked down our long dark driveway, and placed the garbage can by our mailbox on the lampless road. A man had just left Tinky's Tavern at the other end of the street. He didn't stop the car after it hit my father's body.

I didn't know this happened until hours later, after the Life Flight helicopter landed in our front yard and woke me up, after my grandparents took me into their arms and then their car. The helicopter lights were so bright. The sound was so loud. It was so, so loud. Mom went to the hospital to see if Daddy would live long enough to make it worth the rest of the family coming as well. He did. He didn't die, but he was on life support. So that first night, the whole family huddled in the waiting room, doing just that: waiting.

I was four. I remember the faces of adults not knowing how to comfort me. I remember fluorescent lights. I remember how far away the lightning bugs felt. What would our lawn be now?

———————

It will be months before my father is conscious again. While he is still in the coma, we take all the money our neighbors raised at the benefit in the VFW hall to install a ramp over the stairs to the door of our house and to buy a van that could fit a wheelchair. The rest of the money—from selling his beloved powder-blue GTO convertible—goes to hospital bills. Despite this, his mother (Frances, technically my grandmother, although I never call her that), believes my mother has gotten rich off the accident. She and my mom barely talk throughout any of this and when they do, it's often fighting about the best way to take care of my dad. One night, when Daddy is still in the hospital, Mom gets drunk and walks into our front yard. Around the same time, my grandparents (Mom's mom and stepdad) are dropping me off after I've spent the day with them. We pull in the driveway and see Mom outside, facing the direction of Frances's home.

"Frances! Oh Frances!" she's yelling.

I run out of the car scared, but like the country moths that collected on our porch light, I cling to her. "Momma what's wrong, what are you doing?" I am still only four years old, maybe five at this point.

My grandparents are right behind me, my grandfather demanding my mom stop yelling, my grandmother calling me back to her. "Presh! Precious, please come here!" Pleading, tears in her voice, she begs me to just walk away from what she knows will become a memory, a trauma ghost, a thing I'll wish I could forget but won't.

I'm whimpering and can't make sense of anything. Mom is now yelling at Frances and also my grandfather. We don't know if it was a neighbor or Frances herself, but someone calls the cops, and this memory is now filled with red and blue lights, of my mom in the back of a cop car and of my grandmother's shirt, which she tries to use to shield my eyes from all of this. But it's too late.

I imagine it was this incident that was Mom's rock bottom. I consider asking her, but I am worried today about triggering her depression. She still lives in shame for the mistakes she's made. I try to tell her we have all made mistakes, and that the healing is the important part of the story, not the trauma. The fact that Mom gets sober and never wavers—that's bigger than this incident. But I can't tell one without the other, and isn't that how it goes?

Mom gets sober seemingly overnight. My Gramps (her dad) tries to get her to join him at his meetings in downtown Cleveland, but there, Mom is surrounded by white businessmen who have no sense of what it would mean to move through recovery as a single parent without money. So, instead of AA, she does it on her own. For me, she'll usually explain. She knew she had to raise me, and so she stopped drinking. Just like that.

When my father finally came out of the coma, we were warned that his brain injury meant he would "never be the same." We were told that he might be violent and aggressive for a period of time. Sometimes nurses had to hold him down in the adult-sized padded crib where he writhed around and occasionally threw punches.

We would make the drive to the Cleveland Metro hospital regularly. From our country road, toward the Goodyear Tire digital billboard that flashed the weather and the time, and adjacent to the city skyline edged with flames. Our olive-green Oldsmobile Delta 88, sometimes an eight-track of Queen playing in the background. "We Are the Champions" was Daddy's racing song; I remember it blaring from the garage, his crew all singing along, and then quietly, me too. But on the way to the hospital, Freddie Mercury sounded like a liar. We'd arrive at the hospital on what always seemed to be gray days. Within months, Daddy was in physical therapy and participating in other activities the hospital had for patients with brain injuries. One day the nurses told me I could join my dad during craft hour. I made a ceramic lion. A round circle with spaghetti strands of clay hair around the outside edges, two eyes, and a smile.

"Mike, do you think Raechel did a good job?" my mom asked him when I finished. "Do you like it?"

My dad looked at it and scowled. "No," he said simply, and turned his head away.

Flushed with embarrassment, I looked toward my mom for help, but saw that her eyes were glassy and wet. She turned away from both of us for a moment, then grabbed me by the shoulders and pulled me into a hug, whispering, "He doesn't mean it, peanut, he doesn't know what he's saying."

It would be like that for the year he would live with us after leaving the hospital. Mom was sober and ready, or at least ready to try, to take care of both of us. She became expert at navigating sharp corners while pushing him in the chair, and built impressive arm strength hoisting him in and out of the van, pushing him up the ramp and into the house. I was too young and small to be of any use in these physical endeavors, and too young, really, to be of any use in the emotional ones either. I was scared of my father most of those days. The doctors told Mom he would likely continue to be physically aggressive. At four years old, I watched him flail violently in his wheelchair, unaware of his surroundings. It was as though whatever sense of his old self was left inside was fighting like a boxer against the damaged brain and body he newly occupied.

On the first Christmas after the accident, we go to Cloverleaf—which is a racetrack when it's warm and a Christmas tree lot when it's cold—and Mom pushes the wheelchair through the snow-covered dirt. We get help from our neighbor, Dave, getting the tree into the house. Daddy sits in his wheelchair in the living room watching it all unfold. It's hard to say if he remembers the year before, when we went to pick out a tree together, when he hoisted it over his shoulders and tied it to the top of our car, and then when he took me in his hands and lifted me up to put the star on top. I think he must remember, because the day Dave brings the tree in the house, Dad is angry. I can sense this, and I try to appease him. It isn't right, but most of us end up talking to him the way people talk to children. His head injury doesn't make him a child, but none of us—even the doctors—know exactly how to communicate, and so we resort to infantilizing. I am five years old.

In grad school, decades later, I meet a short-haired Scorpio dyke who will become a sister, and who also has a brain injury. Hers is very, very different from my father's, but she knows about cars that break your body and your brain. When I tell her it's like my father died, she grimaces. I can tell that wasn't the correct thing to say. She teaches me about critical disability studies, about how my father's brain isn't the problem, the society who can't accommodate it is. To say he's died is dehumanizing, says my Scorpio. He is still him, just in a different way, and we should blame the medical industrial complex, not his inability to be a father in the way we're taught fathers are supposed to be. I think of him bored in a nursing home and no one knowing how best to support him, and I know that she is right. And also—I'm sorry, but it's like my father died.

There was no critical disability studies on the racetrack. No disability justice movement that we knew to tap into (although it did exist), and certainly no images of low-income adults with disabilities in pop culture. We were really on our own to figure out how to be with him, how to talk to and about him. I landed on a lot of pity—for my dad, of course, but also for my mom. I don't have a lot of memories of feeling sorry for myself; that came later. At this point, I felt that my role was to tend.

———————

"Daddy, do you want to hang up an ornament?" I ask tentatively, showing him the box we brought down from the attic, full of a mix of handmade and store-bought decorations.

There's a pause. And then: "NO!" he shouts. "NO!" he flails in his chair. It rocks, I think he'll tip over. I cover my eyes in panic.

"Momma," I whimper and run over to her.

"Mike, what's wrong?!" Mom rushes to him. She holds his arms down.

He calms down quickly. Mom is still holding his arms when she looks around for me. I'm sitting huddled behind the tree, using it as a bit of a shield.

She tries to triage. "Honey, why don't you set up the Nativity?" Her husband is calm; what task can she put her daughter on to distract from what's just happened?

I nod silently and go retrieve the dolls we picked to represent Mary, Joseph, and Jesus—Kid Sister, My Buddy, and a Black baby doll my grandmother got me, respectively. Mom wasn't religious, but Gramps and Nana were, and so we'd go to church on holidays and it was easier for everyone if we just played more by the rules. To be honest though, I think Mom mostly encouraged it as an opportunity to talk about racist depictions of Jesus. "Jesus wasn't white," she told me every year when we placed the Black doll in the manger, "so Dr. Baby is perfect." I named it Dr. Baby because my pediatrician was Black and I didn't know any other Black people. I'm not saying this isn't fucked up, but there was a period of time when I honestly thought all Black people were doctors.

The Nativity is set and Daddy is calm. We hear water from a pot boil into a spill—we have no teapot, so we heat up the water in a soup pan to mix with the Swiss Miss hot chocolate packs we buy on sale. Mom, shaking, pours water in a mug, mixing with a spoon. "Whipped cream, peanut?" she asks, catching her breath from the kitchen. "Yes, please," I say, staring quizzically and fearfully at my father, who is looking off in the distance the way he usually does now. I twirl the side of my hair in a pattern that becomes so compulsive I later develop a bald spot. *Twirl twirl pull . . . twirl twirl pull.* The Reddi-wip whirls.

———————

During the year that Daddy lived with us, I would often hear Mom crying in the bedroom or the bathroom. Sometimes I would go to her, try to comfort her. Sometimes I made it worse, sometimes better. She was either glad for me, someone to hold close and love, or she was devastated by me, a symbol of her failed motherhood. *What kind of mother lets her daughter see her fall apart like this?* I imagine she asked herself.

Before the accident, my dad raced stock cars. I'd grow up to learn that this was a marker of being white trash, and at one point I'd attach it to shame, but when I was young, it made me very proud. I'd get to go to the races sometimes and watch him drive in circles around the dirt track. I loved the black-and-white checkered flags. (I'd have an affinity for that pattern in clothes and bedroom décor for most of my life.) I was shy, but I also loved the attention I got for being my dad's daughter.

"See your Daddy out there? He gonna win you a trophy," grown-ups in the stands would tell me between sips of frothy beer in crinkled plastic cups. Their voices were always slightly muffled because of the earplugs Mom would adorn me with before arriving at the track. In response, I'd blush shyly and silently nuzzle into Mom's soft and ample hip. I felt very special.

On Sunday mornings, Daddy's race car crew would come over to eat breakfast, watch NASCAR (or, when my mom could get away with changing the channel, *Little House on the Prairie*), and drink beer. There wasn't a lot of censoring that went on in our house. Appropriateness, decorum, protecting young children from "language" wasn't really on the radar of the adults who filled our Tinkers Creek home. So I would overhear swear words, lewd jokes, sometimes racist comments. Mom would always interject when any of the men said anything racist, though. She had no patience for that. And so there I witnessed, on a very small scale, the nuance of "the white working-class."

———

It's not wrong that poor, white America has its share of bigots, but it's also not that simple. "Those who live in the most dire circumstances possess a complex and oftentimes contradictory humanity and subjectivity," theorist Avery F. Gordon writes, "that is never adequately glimpsed by viewing them as victims or, on the other hand, as superhuman agents." Gordon describes this as the "complex personhood" that means oppressed groups "suffer graciously and selfishly too, get stuck in the symptoms of their troubles and also transform themselves." Indeed, Mom made mistakes, but she was also the victim of a capitalist system, and later, ageism and sexism. Some of our neighbors struggled with addiction, but they were also hard workers. Mom didn't graduate from high school, but her justice-driven heart gave me an example of who understood, on an intrinsic level, the notion of solidarity. Daddy's race car crew, largely, didn't understand that—so instead of feeling a sense of commonality with others who were being harmed by the system, they felt a sense of threat. We were as full of contradictions as any community you can think of.

I also had a foot in another world. Some of us do. My working-class family was full of "backwards" and artless low-brow conversation and antics, but at the same time, I had grandparents who loved the arts and were good with money in a way that allowed them to travel and take me to plays and museums. It was not uncommon for me to spend an afternoon drinking root beer in my dad's garage, Metallica blaring in the background, surrounded by pictures of tan white women in bikinis bending over muscle cars, and then later spend an evening at an upscale restaurant with my grandparents, who taught me which fork to use for each course of a meal.

But in my memories, the first four years of my life were an even keel of white trash banality: race cars, beer-drinking men covered in car grease, and the women who loved them. I loved them too, and would continue to love them, in different ways, throughout my life. To me, at that impressionable age, these were the men who took care of things—these men who embodied the same kind of hegemonic masculinity I would later deconstruct in academic feminist essays. These were the heroes. I'm not supposed to say this, but this was what I needed and this was what I lost.

In their place, my heroes became the women who survived despite men's absence. Whether the men were taken from homes by car accidents or jail or a restraining order, by the time I was five, I was surrounded almost entirely by resilient women. My own coven of persistent Lampyridae, those lightning bugs fighting with persistent glow against the odds. They drank beer and swore. Their clothes were too big or too small. Many of them were tattooed. And always, always, in their glorious excess, they showed up.

2.
The Coven of Persistent Lampyridae

Aunty Bun is the name I give to Robin, my mom's best friend from high school. She lives in Virginia, but she visits often to see her mom and my mom. Sometimes we go to Virginia, or meet in West Virginia, and in any case, Mom and Robin laugh so much anytime they're together, and I play with Robin's three kids, who are all beautiful, with olive skin and luscious curly hair they get from their father, who is Iraqi. But Aunty Bun is white like Mom, and big in every way: tall, round, loud. She dyes her hair blonde and feathers her bangs. She is confident in a way sometimes Mom isn't, and she talks about sex and swears. Most of our visits involve sitting around someone's kitchen table, sometimes playing a game, always eating. I love our visits with Aunty Bun, and I love that, especially after Daddy's accident, visits with her seem to bring a lightness to Mom. They are, together, high school girlfriends again, speaking sometimes in inside jokes and a language that is all their own.

I see this all around me. The women at the racetrack, or at the bars where I perch with ginger ales, or the ones I see at Kmart in short-shorts and crop tops sorting through their cash, a credit card, and a check to make sure they cover the cost of their purchase. They are different from the Strathmore moms I see at school—the ones who live in the fancy development that rests on a hill at the top of the valley. More of their skin shows, they laugh louder, they take up space in a way that I will only later notice attracts judgmental stares. I am mired in and mesmerized by them and the way they somehow embody what is outside the lines. How does their skin hold all that is frenetic?

Tina is another race car driver's wife, and her hair is huge. Crimped and teased and covered in hairspray. She always wears her black leather jacket, worn and weathered from the air of countless motorcycle rides, and covered in strips of black leather fringe. She smokes. She cheers louder than anyone at the racetrack. She is so cool, I find myself thinking often.

Rita, our neighbor and mother to Evie and Julian, had a rose tattoo on her wrist. I admired it as it passed from her chin to ear, back and forth, along with the cigarette dangling from her fingers. She had a voice like the sound of bicycle tires on grainy dirt and her laugh went from throaty to high-pitched, usually followed by a smoker's cough. She came over when things at her home were either very good or very bad. I preferred when things were very good, when she and Mom would play cards at the table, and I would get to play with Evie, who was two years older than me, and Julian, who was two years younger than me.

I always roped Evie into making potions with me. Magic spells for love, for days off school, for the tree in the front yard to grow so high we could climb it to the clouds. Mom would lay out towels on the kitchen floor, followed by mixing bowls, Kool-Aid packs, water, food coloring, and anything else I could grab without her protest. Purple sugar, green sugar, orange droplets from the tiny plastic tube, stirring while puffs of powder covered our faces. Mixing, mixing, mixing, cackling the way we'd heard the Wicked Witch of the West do on TV, both of us believing something must come true.

The other times Rita came over, when things were very bad, she'd almost always be crying. Sobbing, really. Usually still smoking. These were the times when Dan would hit her. I'd witnessed it a couple times, but for the most part, I only saw the aftermath. A black-and-blue eye. A bloody lip. Fading pink handprints on her throat.

"Go play in your room," Mom would tell me. I would herd Evie and Julian out of the kitchen, where Mom would stay to take care of her neighbor.

These women like Rita, Aunty Bun, the women at the racetrack, and Mom, of course, were the earliest images I had of the malleable borders of femininity. I didn't come out as a queer femme until I was nineteen, but it is clear to me now how deeply I was shaped by the excesses of the community that raised me. The tattoos, the trashy clothes, the sex for pleasure and survival. The strength.

3.
Sunshine on the Water Looks So Lovely

A few years after the accident, Frances took custody of my father and filed for his divorce with my mom. A couple years after that, she also took the house we had been a family in, and all the money from it. In exchange, the government sent Mom a few hundred dollars a month for her dependent (me) and Frances got Daddy's disability benefits. We got nothing from the man who hit my father.

———————

But at first we are still in our house, and when my father moves out, things get logistically easier—Mom only has to get one person dressed, bathed, fed, and safely in a car. Emotionally, it is more fraught. Having more time gives her more room to think. Specifically, about what a mess her life has become and how she is going to raise a daughter on her own. She no longer has her waitressing job at the Brown Derby and we are living on the part-time pay and measly benefits from her office job. We still have hospital debt, plus all that we accrued in trying to accommodate my dad's physical disability—a new-to-us van that fit his chair, the shower bench, the ramp up our front steps. But even with all that, it's only me now that mom is responsible for.

Within a year, Keith moves in. Keith is young, in his late twenties, and he had worked on my dad's race car crew. He's tall, with a thin frame and a round belly. His hair is curly and unkempt and he wears big glasses with silver frames. He's childlike and silly and will often switch into different voices mid-sentence. He was broke and could no longer afford rent and we needed some levity. It was the kind of deal poor folks made with one another, mutual exchanges based on necessity, but also a surrender to spiteful pleasure. We'd find ways to be joyful, dammit. Without us, Keith was homeless, but he'd make jokes anyway. Without Keith, Mom was a tragic single mother, but she'd laugh anyway.

At the time, I had no idea Keith was gay. In 1991, being gay was not exactly widely accepted, and for a guy who hung out with white race car drivers, being gay was impossible. He was deeply closeted; Mom was one of the only people who knew. They didn't tell me for multiple reasons, I assume, but primarily because a six-year-old couldn't be trusted to not let something slip. But there were signs, and looking back, it's so clear.

"My favorite New Kid on the Block is Jordan, but Julian says he's gay," I remember saying in the living room to Mom and Keith, flipping my Jordan Knight pillow from one side to the other. I pause while they shift uncomfortably, and then, "What's gay?"

They shoot furtive glances toward one another. "Well, technically, gay means happy," my mom says.

"But that's not what they mean," I challenge.

"Gay's not bad," Mom says quickly, glancing at Keith again, who is now wiping beads of sweat from his forehead.

"Hmm," I say not satisfied, but I drop it and return to watching TV, my head resting on the bright blue and purple pillow, my cheek against the screenprint of Jordan Knight's face.

———

It wouldn't be confirmed that Keith was gay until I was twelve, trapped in a stairwell by my mom's boyfriend, Ron.

"I don't want to live here, please let me go, I don't want to be here, I want to go home," I was crying, trapped, terrified, bravely stating what was true to a man who had put me in this position so many times before.

"You know why your mom won't let you go home?" he slurred. "Because Keith is a faggot and all of his faggot magazines and dildos are all over the house."

He stared at me with his shark eyes. He knew he had just revealed a secret; he knew I'd be caught off guard. I put the pieces together. I had actually seen the magazines he'd referenced. I think I vaguely made sense of it, but I also assumed porn was just a mix of men with men, women with women, and so it wasn't until Ron spat this out that I realized with certainty that Keith was like my great Aunt Eunice, the only other gay person I knew in real life.

Years later, Mom and I talk openly about Keith, if he is dating, and how his drag performances are going. Good, she tells me, he's happy, she thinks. But, she mentions, *No one at his new job knows he's gay, just in case you're ever at the store.* I am astounded sometimes with how very fast progress can move, and how at the same time, the struggles are exactly the same.

———————

Keith had a brother named Lenny who also couldn't afford rent, so at one point he lived in our basement. He had a ferret, which I was excited about. Lenny was skinny, blonde, wore backward baseball hats and usually no shirt. He'd babysit sometimes. Another poor people deal: watch my kid, not because you're qualified, but because I have no one else and because you owe me.

Lenny loosely monitors me, Evie, and Julian when we go to the creek to catch crawfish. We never catch any in the creek behind our house—they are further down, in the deeper part of the water—but we try anyway. On our way through the woods, we step on branches that crack underneath our feet, we sing-song nonsense, we tumble with the abandon of children who don't understand the weight of their lives. Julian is sometimes barefoot. Evie and I join him once we reach the water. We let our toes cool in the stream. We place our hands against the wet earth and we wait. Evie gets bored and tries skipping rocks. Julian tries to go deeper in the current. I stay, squinting in the reflection of the sun against the ripples. I breathe. The water is traveling past my tiny knuckles, wet and smooth, and I am still.

Lenny has been asked to pick up pet food from Wilson's Feed Mill. He realizes how late it is and tells us we have to go. We are all resistant.

"I don't care about you two, your mom didn't put me in charge, but you," Lenny says pointing at me, "have to come with me or my brother will be pissed."

I'm frustrated, but also, at this point, still a rule follower. "Bye Evie, bye Julian," I say shaking my hands of the water and following Lenny back through the woods to our driveway and into the beat-up car he drives.

"We need cat food," he says. "And ferret food."

Wilson's Feed Mill is just around the corner, sitting on the edge of the canal. We park next to a semi that's unloading big bags of horse feed into the storage silos. We walk in and Lenny searches for what we need. That day, the mill is active, the feed is being processed. It stops me on the front porch of the store. I stare at the silos, pouring out a waterfall of what looks like sawdust, a cascade, an abundance that I find glorious and hypnotizing.

Summer days in the valley were the closest thing I had to religion. The shattered-glass water in the creek, the abundance of the mill, running like the wind was carrying me against an earth full of bones. It was awe and repentance, holy baptism washing the soles of my dirty feet. It was daydreaming that felt real for survival. It was all sacred ritual, inadvertent and weightless as grace.

I don't know how much time has passed, but eventually Lenny is back out with two bags of food. "Let's go," he says.

4.

"Otherwise, I am fine": Ghosts of Tinkers Creek / Specters of the Canal

Tinkers Creek is off of Canal Road, which means we pass the Ohio and Erie Canal every single day. When we get a rainstorm in the valley, the canal nearly always floods. At least one group of boys or men will take a raft out onto the street, paddling through the rising waters, as the rest of us scoop out our basements with children's pails and buckets from our garages and toolsheds. When the water is calm, it is brown, surrounded by a mess of trees and wild weeds.

Water is organic, and bodies are too, but the depths of many of our canals, our lakes, our rivers—someone had to make them. The Ohio and Erie was made primarily by Irish immigrants, digging and dying for a flask of whiskey and thirty cents a day. The impetus behind the canal was, largely, to make rich men richer: state representative Alfred Kelley wanted a cheap way to transport goods between Lake Erie and the Ohio River. And so he put to work immigrants who used picks and shovels to break 308 miles of earth, and who hauled and hoisted and hurled large sandstone rock to create locks for the water. Many of them died, their immune systems broken from twelve-hour days, easy targets for malaria (what they called "canal fever"). According to Cleveland's National Park Service, "an Irishman was buried for every mile of canal constructed."

I think about those bodies like rungs of a ladder, lined up beneath the soil of the land where I sunk my bare toes. I think about their banal sacrifice, the expectation that one would work from dusk until the dawn and likely catch a fever that would leave you dead. That the hardline of negotiation was whiskey, because anything better was unrealistic, and how else could you cope?

In 1819, an Irish worker named Timothy Geoghegan wrote a letter to his sister: "I don't know, dear Sister, if any of us will survive, but God willing, we will live to see a better day. Six of me tentmates died this very day and were stacked like cordwood until they could be taken away. Otherwise, I am fine."

There is actually a cemetery on Tinkers Creek, hidden in the woods a mile or so from where I grew up, that is said to be full of Irish bodies. Native bodies too. The only graves, though, belong to white settlers (which, in the early nineteenth century, didn't include the Irish).

And so there is earth, and the bodies of indigenous people who were killed and buried in split logs, and then above them the bodies of the Irish, and then more soil, and above that, the bodies in caskets of white people with a little more money, and graves that give them names eternal.

I have Irish in my blood, although I don't think I'm of any familial relation to these workers. But I feel them, in this history, in my memory of how the air in Valley View always felt just a little bit thick with spirits. And I certainly feel them as the roots of my convictions; knowing I was reared on the bones of exploited labor is maybe just as significant as being parented by an exploited laborer.

There is another ghost I only just learned about as an adult who I hope maybe also haunts me. Her name was Mary, but I believe she would have chosen differently if she could have. Historical documents describe her as a "cross-dressing pig farmer" who was eccentric but agreeable. She lived in the house that later would be occupied by a wealthy white family called the Gleesons, then eventually owned by the Wingenfelds. Prior to that, the barn was home to the suicide of a boy I went to school with. But this person, who I think if she had been lucky to live in a different era would maybe identify as butch, existed just a few houses from me. I think about her strong hands, wearing overalls that she wasn't supposed to wear, a quiet queer without community or the language for it, feeling closer to her pigs than other humans. In my construction of her—from the sparse details I have—I start to develop a crush. How gentle she must've been. How much I would have liked to kiss her.

When I am thirty, I visit home for Christmas and go inside the house where she lived. I had ordered some flowers from Meghan, the daughter of the Wingenfelds who lives there part-time, who was a year younger than me in school, and who I like very much. We don't talk about Mary, but we talk about ghosts. About the boy we knew who took his life. About how she feels spirits there. And also about the night of my dad's accident.

"I've never told you this," she begins, "but my mom was the one who found your dad after he was hit by the car."

I had no idea. I feel the wind knocked out of me.

"It's actually what made her want to become a nurse," she says. "That night changed her life."

Meghan and I weren't particularly close in school, but after learning this about her mom, I feel uniquely close to her. Both of our moms touched my dad's body that night. It feels . . . significant.

The Gleeson/pig farmer/Wingenfeld house is the first house on Tinkers Creek. Our house was in the middle. The bar, Tinky's Tavern, where the man who hit my father got drunk that night, is at the very end. And all in between are the ladder rungs of dead Irish workers and the bones of erased Native families. Somewhere the ground is stained with my father's blood-mixed-with-car-oil, and with the screams of my mom, and the moment Meghan's mom knew she had to help save lives. It's all swirling about with the pain of my closeted caretaker, and the pain of the pig farmer who I wished I could have kissed.

You're not imagining it: the Valley is full of ghosts.

5.
A Girl Can Do What She Wants to Do

I may have had a crush on Lenny. I tended to have crushes on older boys. Adult men too. My first celebrity crush was Fred Savage, but my second was Jeremy Irons. Fred was age appropriate—he was just a few years older than me when I watched him on *The Wonder Years*. But Jeremy, who I discovered first as the voice of Scar in *The Lion King*, and then in *Die Hard with a Vengeance*, was solidly in his fifties. He could have been my grandfather, but I was wooed.

As a child, my clichéd daddy issues manifested themselves primarily through longing for unattainable celebrities, but by the time I got to college I realized I could start acting on those impulses. And I did. (Like with the thirty-something English professor who asked me to go to a burlesque show, who grabbed my eighteen-year-old hand and placed it on his erection during the performance, who took me home to his studio apartment in Chicago and talked to me about his skin-care regimen right before and a little bit during jerking off on my ass, and then as I was leaving that night, handed me a copy of *Discipline and Punish*, and how as terrible and tropey as he and the whole thing was, and as fucked up as a particular version of feminism would demand it to be, I felt so fucking powerful in his wanting of me, especially because I didn't particularly want him back. Somewhere between the movies and the sex-just-because, I found more playfulness than pathology in these exchanges.)

But before that, it was a lot of fantasy, made more real by the movies I'd watch.

I am seven. Mom and her friend Patty are in the kitchen playing Yahtzee. The room is a little dark because a lightbulb in the overhead fixture is burned out. I am in the living room, stretched out on the carpet, watching television, straining to sort the dialogue in the movie from the rolling dice on the table. *Poison Ivy* is on HBO, which we've figured out how to steal. Drew Barrymore (Ivy) is seducing an older man in the film and I am in awe of it. During a sex scene I decide is too mature for me, I walk into the kitchen. Back then, I played excessively by the rules, self-monitoring myself and censoring what I watched even when my mom didn't.

There is a big open can of black olives on the table. Mom and Patty switch between cigarette hits, olive reaching, and dice rolling.

"Hi, peanut," Mom says when I walk in.

I sit by her and look at the scorecard. She's losing.

"You wanna roll this one?" she asks, handing me the red plastic cup.

I nod and roll.

"Yahtzee!" we both exclaim, earnestly thrilled.

Patty throws up her arms, "You must be good luck, no fair!"

I smile, happy to have helped Mom.

"I'm gonna go finish the movie," I tell them, fishing an olive out of the jar and sending my finger through its hollow center. Mom and Patty keep playing the game. I eat the olive off my finger and give Mom a quick hug. This is not uncommon, for us to exchange hugs just to go to the other room. I think sometimes I just need to be sure of her. To feel her softness against all that was so hard. I think she felt the same of me.

When I go back to the living room, Drew Barrymore and Tom Skerritt are finished fucking and now Ivy is on a rampage. I mentally added her to my list of role models.

———————

Crazy, broken, seductive women were all over early '90s films: Winona Ryder in anything, but especially *Welcome Home Roxy Carmichael*, in which she played a mentally unstable teen who misguidedly believes her mother is a celebrity. Susan Sarandon and Geena Davis's righteous criminality in *Thelma & Louise*. Angelina Jolie's early roles in *Gia* and *Playing by Heart*, both of which featured her as simultaneously deeply damaged and irresistibly sexy. I think I knew, even before desire made sense to me, that I wanted to be sexy, and I think I knew, even before I really knew why, that I was damaged. Or at least that I'd be perceived as damaged. And so these stories of broken women finding their way—even with wreckage in their wake—were entirely aspirational.

Later, I did not want the attention of my mom's boyfriend, but it will happen anyway.

6.
Luckiest People in the World

At one point Keith steals money from us. Mom finds out, and I manage to figure it out, too. It's tense for a while, but eventually we go on like nothing happened. The difference between stealing and borrowing money is ultimately insignificant. Mom never expects anyone she lends money to to actually pay it back. It hurts her feelings that Keith stole instead of "borrowed," but the material result is the same. We move on. If we didn't, we'd be out of a babysitter.

We practiced transformative justice—a term I would learn decades later in activist spaces to describe an alternative approach to the prison system, and generally, to our culture of punishment—without even realizing it. I was taught, very early, that there are not "good people" and "bad people," but rather, there are people who make choices in order to survive. You learn, as organizer Danielle Sered puts it, that "no one enters violence for the first time by committing it." Sometimes that means breaking the law. Sometimes that means doing something you'd really rather not do, that may hurt yourself or people you love, but sometimes you feel like you have no choice. Sometimes you're able to make better decisions than other times. What I learned is that life is hard and we're all doing the best we can with what we have with where we're at.

This is why forgiveness has come easy to me. It's why I don't really even blame Keith for stealing that money. It's why I couldn't possibly stay mad at my mother.

There is no room to cut out someone who messes up when people who mess up are all you've got. You learn that bad decisions don't mean toxic people. If you're lucky, you learn the messy work of healing. And if not, you master the art of compartmentalizing. And then you move the fuck forward and figure out how to pay the gas bill that month.

But even in the midst of this, there are moments when things feel good and sometimes even normal, or at least what I presume is normal, based on my observations of my two-parent, middle-class friends' households. Mom finds a steady job working in a cafeteria at a lighting company in a town just about ten minutes away from our house. Keith helps out with rides to school and packing lunches. And Mom becomes an excellent party planner.

My birthdays, both before and after the accident, were always creative, joyous fun. Once she rented out the Valley View Town Hall, filled it with an array of my favorite homemade and store-bought snacks—pigs in a blanket made from hot dogs and Pillsbury crescent roll dough, crackers and Cheez Whiz from the bottle, to name two—and hung a handmade piñata from the ceiling. This was the birthday the year after the accident. She worked so hard to help me smile. And I did.

"One!" the room of children from school and the neighborhood and their parents shouted as Mom spun me around blindfolded. "Two!" Mom spun me again. "Three!"

I swung the plastic bat toward the decoupaged globe. One swing and the candy rained down. I shrieked with delight and Mom did too as she lifted the blindfold away from my eyes and released me to the candy pile, joining my young friends in our quest to gather as much sugar as possible. The parents clapped. Mom did well.

And even in the confines of our always-messy house, that always smelled faintly of cat piss, that we had to work really hard to make fit for any company that wasn't our neighbors, there were moments of deep joy. We played music a lot. We sang a lot. We laughed a lot. Despite it all, we laughed, we laughed.

I am lying on the old, puke-brown couch with holes all over it, in my favorite Spuds MacKenzie baseball T-shirt, surrounded by junk and disaster, but I am holding the petal-pink collector's edition of *Barbra Streisand's Greatest Hits* in my hands, gazing up at the lyric book as "People" plays loudly from the stereo. Uncle Dana got the disc set for Mom for Christmas, and we wear it out. Mom got her love of musicals from her mom (my grandmother, Ammie), and our love of musicals is another thing that I will only later learn is not something people generally associate with the kind of place I grew up.

"*People who need PEOPLE!*" Mom enters the room as the crescendo hits.

Our dog, Bear, is alarmed by our sudden burst of activity. I sit up and rub his ears and join Mom. Somewhat organically, we both begin to change the lyrics to, "*Puppies, puppies who need other puppies, are the luckiest puppies in the world!*" We sing this to our dog and will continue singing it to Bear, and then to Roxy who we get years later, and I will share that story with my partner Logan when I sing to our Captain, and I will remember how perfect and normal it was, even though we could hardly pay the bills, and how, probably later that day Mom cried or we fought, for a moment I was just a kid who sang Barbra with her mom, no matter that our living room seemed unfit conditions for the clean, petal-pink CD case. We still had the music.

Four years after the accident, when I was in second grade, we even went to Disney World. Mom saved all the money she would have spent on cigarettes, and a year after she gave up smoking, we smashed the Mickey Mouse piggy bank and drove nearly sixteen hours to Florida, listening to *The Bodyguard* soundtrack on repeat. We found discounted tickets through a condo share program that we fully intended to scam. Keith went with us, sang louder to Whitney than any of us, and for five glorious days, we played a normal family on vacation.

I got Daddy a souvenir that I'd bring to him at Frances's house, where I'd visit him about once a month. This is when things felt less normal. I learned very young how to manage adults. I knew that Frances would say negative things about my mom and I knew that I would have to stay quiet in response. I knew that Daddy would only remember certain things and that he would be depressed. I knew that I had to stay upbeat. Even at six, seven, eight years old, I tried to perform to make everyone more comfortable than I was.

"Hi, Daddy," I said, sitting down at Frances's Formica kitchen table, breathing through my mouth to avoid inhaling what felt like decades of undusted counters and unwashed carpet. "I brought you this from Disney World."

"Disney World? If your mother has enough money for that, I don't know why you need child support from the government," Frances spat at me.

"Your mom sold my tools," Daddy half-shouted, the way he did after the accident, about to report what he'd been brainwashed with. "She must have a lot of money."

Tears burned my eyes, but I had to find something to say to make it less awkward. "Well, she saved a lot of money and we got discounts on the tickets. And . . ." I glanced down at the thrift store shoes I was wearing, recalling the "PAST DUE" printed in all caps on an envelope on our counter. "Well, we're not rich, Daddy."

Neither my grandmother nor my father would ask me any questions during these visits. I learned to volunteer information, to not be hurt by the lack of interest, to talk to my father the way I hoped he'd talk to me. *How was your day? Did you build that model car, I love it! Do you like how the trees are changing colors this week?*

I did my time. I'd keep the visits short. I didn't know, I still don't know, how to behave with him. I didn't know, and I still don't know, how to not let it affect me that he can't be caring toward me the way I long for.

It's not his fault. I wonder how much more, or what differently, I could do. I don't know the answer to this.

7.

A Memory before the Accident

Daddy is quiet and uncomfortable at my grandmother's house. Well, at least he is quiet, this I remember for sure, but my memory of his affect is less certain. Am I projecting that on to him today? Am I constructing an image of my father that is more archetypal than real? The stoic working-class race car driver, uncomfortable with the particularities of middle-class decorum—did he know how to hold his fork, did he remember to wear a tie when he was supposed to? (Did he own a tie?) I know I'll have to ask my mom for more details about who he was, but I don't want to. The conversations about my dad are always survival based. What can I ask without breaking down, what can she answer without breaking down? How can we talk about something deeply personal and devastating while keeping it light enough to function? We've found a balance, but it doesn't get us very far.

In what I remember though, or at least in what I think I do, my dad is quiet and shifting in a chair, grateful for the can of beer that allows him to do something with his hands. I remember sitting on his lap a lot. Holding me with one hand, and a beer with the other, are the times I imagine my father was most comfortable in social situations. I have so little to grasp when it comes to any semblance of making him proud, so I hold on to this as a victory. I like to think I was a bit of a security blanket for him.

How badly we both needed each other to feel safe. How deeply we have failed each other since.

In this memory, my grandmother asks him something, a question he doesn't know quite how to answer, so Mom steps in to help. He's grateful for the assistance and takes another sip of beer, squeezing me tight around my waist.

There are pictures of this. Of me on his lap while he drinks a beer. In one picture, I'm wearing a hunter-green floral dress with a white lace collar. It's my birthday and he's just gifted me two guinea pigs. I hold one for the picture, the flash turns the rodent's eyes red. My dad is half-smiling and I look absolutely content and also a little proud. I am collapsed into him, and although this memory is fuzzier outside the picture, I do recall feeling glad for Daddy and my new pets. Smug even. *What a Daddy I have! I am the luckiest girl.* The chair is big and soft. I sink back against his chest and the smoky fabric. His beard is so full, and it smells like Camels and Coors. Sour and ashy and perfect.

8.
I Don't Belong Here

In my mind, we are white trash until I am roughly eight years old. But at that point, around 1993, suddenly the world is bigger than Tinkers Creek. I spend more time with my grandparents (Mom's mom and stepdad) in a suburb called Independence, with my other grandparents (Mom's dad and stepmom) in Sagamore Hills, and with my uncle in Cleveland Heights. These were moments of respite. My grandparents and my uncle were always more well-off than Mom and me. Their houses were clean, they discussed literature, movies, and politics. They didn't talk like our neighbors.

Gramps and Nana's condo in Sagamore Hills is small, but full of knickknacks that look expensive, and they both dress professionally for work. Nana is always adorned with big necklaces, sometimes a bracelet on the one wrist she has left—Nana lost her arm from cancer, long before I was born. None of the grandkids are fazed by her one arm, which she occasionally braces with a prosthetic; it's all we've known of her. Her nails are always perfect—she goes to the salon and brings the prosthetic with her, places it on the table while the technician works on her attached hand and then the other. Nana has a beautiful mix of confidence and vulnerability. By the time I know her, she is well into the acceptance phase of the loss of her arm, but she still likes to hide her "stump," as she calls it, in pictures. She has all the energy of a fiercely independent woman, but simultaneously lives out, unapologetically and tenderly, the reality of the way we all need one another. She asks Gramps to cut her food, she asks one of the grandkids to hold the wine bottle while she pulls the cork, and if she can't grab a handrail on the stairs, she'll ask for your shoulder.

She is also positive, sometimes shockingly so, in the face of obstacles—pain, illness, changes in plans: "It is what it is," she'll say with a shrug, "I'm still very blessed." Today, Nana is the only grandparent I have left, and she is exactly the same. So powerfully herself, so tenaciously grateful, and an absolute testimony to how life could be if we were just more willing to share in the work.

When I learn the word "charming," I will think of Gramps, who I recognize even as a small child is a smooth talker, someone who makes you feel lucky to be getting his attention. His laugh fills a room. At a table, he leans back in his chair, with one arm stretched toward the table, fingers tapping rhythmically as he listens, then turning still when he speaks. He seems like a businessman, and I will learn when I get older that he's in public relations. I'm impressed by him. His hair is so stylish for an older man: thick, white, and side-parted with a wave in his bangs. His nose is big, prominent. He's been sober since Mom was a teenager. He is a believer in the Program, and a lover of Cleveland. A thick coffee-table book about the city is displayed proudly in their home and Gramps flips through the pages with me, telling stories about this building or that moment in history. He was proud of his city, and I was too, but mostly I was proud of him. Proud to be his granddaughter.

Ammie and Daddad's home in Independence has an entirely different energy. It is small, but feels big to me, and it is deeply comforting. It's clean but cluttered, also adorned with knickknacks, but ones that have a lot more history—model ships that Daddad made by hand, dusty old Shakespeare plays on the bookshelves, a basket of *Playbills* from the Playhouse or Playhouse Square where they go to the theater. The coffee table has piles of library books: novels for Ammie, history books for Daddad. It is cozy, but also antique. You are careful not to break the Revolutionary War figurine you walk past, but also you can collapse on the couch and curl up in a blanket without a second thought. I love the mix of this. For years we have dinner there every Sunday in the dining room, then more frequently on TV trays in the living room. And for all of elementary school and some of middle school, Fridays are designated "Ammie days"—she will pick me up from school, we will head straight to the library and collect books and a VHS for the night. We will read, we will craft, she will give me prompts to write about on construction paper or sometimes type on the typewriter that lived in their closet. She always knew I was a writer.

In the evening, Ammie will shower and prepare for dinner, which required fancy clothes and a face of makeup— sometimes I'd help, picking out eyeshadows and lipsticks and learning to apply what she called "rouge." Her bedroom vanity smelled like pink clay and peach powder and the perfume counter at the mall; no, that's not quite it, the scent was an *apothecary*. Everything was soft.

Uncle Dana has the biggest house of everyone. A two-story with three bedrooms, beautiful art on the walls, crystals in the window. He pours wine from bottles into carafes and stores his filtered water in beautiful cobalt blue bottles. He has a surround-sound stereo system installed so he can play his new favorite artist loudly, "the way it's supposed to sound." For a while we have the same favorites: Alanis, Fiona, Liz. Around the corner from Coventry Road, he lives the life of a well-off bachelor, and I put him on a bit of a pedestal. He is a lawyer, but will later quit the practice to become a New Age ("New Thought," he'd correct me) minister. He travels. He goes to nice restaurants. He has taught me so much about what I want. And when I am an adult, his home becomes the home where I stay when I go to Cleveland. When Mom is near-homeless and in either a trailer or her friend's spare room and can't host me, I go to Uncle Dana's, in his lofted attic room, where I enjoy his cable TV and treadmill and wine with him at night.

And this, all this in contrast to the constant moving around that we will eventually endure—the evictions, the mess, the cat piss, the unpaid utility bills. Look at these three homes I had in spite of it.

Later I will become an anti-capitalist activist, eventually *another* Marxist PhD and professor, and I will give lessons on these loopholes. I will teach about the history of bootstrapism, the myth of the American Dream. I will talk about how class in many ways is static, but also how it is spatial and temporal, and to do so I will sometimes share just the surface of my story: *My mom lives in a trailer in Ohio now, she's on welfare, but for a long time she wasn't, but before that we were. My grandparents were fine though. And so that's one reason I'm here—because for a period we had enough money to not be on welfare, and because when my mom didn't have the money, my grandparents gave me a $500 check to reserve a dorm room.* As a kid, I knew the deep trenches of white poverty, but it depended on the day, the hour, if I was in the thick of scarcity, or in an intermission from it.

I will say this to wealthy students with wealthy families at a private college on the East Coast, and they will look at me like I am so impressive. *Her mom lives in a trailer*, some of them will say in the hall, *and now she has a PhD!* Many of them will miss the point. I will tell the story again to community college students in the Midwest and they will understand. They know how it works. Some of them are homeless and no one wrote them a check—they just qualified for every scholarship. Some of them have stories just like mine and they will nod. At both schools, I will get approached by the students who are grateful to me for coming out as working-class. In my first year teaching after finishing my PhD, a student at the private college will come up after class with tears in her eyes and say, "My parents shower after work, not before. There's such a difference. Thank you for telling us your story. I feel less alone here now." She will be my first mentee and will go on to lead the first-generation college student group on campus. After she graduates, we will remain friends, we will continue to share stories about knowing how to navigate different worlds. "My mom doesn't understand the whole college thing," she will say over the coffee we share to celebrate her admittance to grad school, "but she's very proud."

———————

We sometimes had to keep secrets from the rest of my family. *Don't tell Ammie that Dan and Rita were fighting in our house. Don't tell Gramps the power got shut off.* Or sometimes less ominous: *Just don't mention to Uncle Dana that Keith took the letter 'f' off Burger King's 'Now Hiring All Shifts' sign.*

I knew the difference between Mom-and-me-family and my broader family. I learned how to code-switch between my own relatives. It would serve me in so many ways after—code-switching from academic to white trash and then back again; code-switching from queer to straight.

At the same time, I begin to connect more with friends from school than from the neighborhood. I begin to notice the differences between my friends who live on Tinkers Creek and my friends who live in Strathmore—a development on top of a hill, placed, it seemed, as a reminder that the residents who had money were superior to those of us who didn't.

Strathmore houses were cookie-cutter two-story homes you'd expect to see in any suburb, but I thought they were beautiful. Even walking upstairs to the bedrooms gave me a rush. There was so much space. The houses were so clean. The parents were so calm. They ate dinner together at a long table. The moms got to stay home. The dads wore suits. Compared to our one-story home, always a disaster, to the yelling that had become commonplace, to the secondhand, trash-picked furniture, to the struggle that hung heavy in our living room air—it was a different country.

By third grade, the contrast made me angry. I was livid at my mom for making me shop at thrift stores. I was furious that she couldn't keep the house clean. I hated that our car broke down, I hated that we were always late. At nine I fought with my mom like a teenager. We both yelled. Screamed, even. Usually, it was me shouting about how I wanted better from her, and her defensively screaming that I was ungrateful. And Mom was, for years, inclined to throw things. Not at me, but someplace to make an impact. She broke hair dryers against walls. Plates in sinks. The fights were loud, violently theatrical. A crescendo of all the rage she had no place to put. The soundtrack of a lost husband, welfare checks, precarious employment. The ambient noise of the Valley was the soft hum of crickets and the raw cries of broken dreams.

And then . . . the fights would end. Usually Mom would be the first to start crying. Then I'd cry. We'd both apologize for what we'd said or done, we'd hug each other until the hugging became holding, we'd resolve to never fight like that again.

Oftentimes this would happen in the van. We'd be running late to something and I'd be scolding her for not being more responsible. *"I'm sorry, I'M SORRY!"* she'd sometimes scream, *"I just won't go at all, why don't you try getting there yourself?!"* I'd sob in the passenger seat while she, also in tears, slammed her hands into the steering wheel. When we'd get to where we were going— my grandparents' house, a school event—we'd sit in the driveway or parking lot, and we'd mend. Hugs into holding, apologies into promises. Always, once we got where we were going, Mom would stay in the car a few more minutes and reapply, or usually apply for the first time, her makeup. Mom, in general, put very little energy into her appearance. Unlike some of our early neighbors, Mom hid her body, rotating between three or four outfits, but she never went without at least lipstick and mascara—even when running late—and usually they would be applied in the mirror above the steering wheel. There were tissues, old receipts, and fast food bags, covered in her blot marks. (Today, in my car too, lipstick prints adorn the garbage in the side door compartment.)

And after, the drive back home would be so full of love. We'd sing along to our favorite cassette tapes—Phil Collins, Whitney Houston, Carole King, Fleetwood Mac. We'd do air drum solos, we'd harmonize. The contrast sounds jarring, but it was just so common, to go from fighting to laughing, shouting to singing, with almost no time in between.

"Well, I've been afraid of changing', cause I built my life around you," Mom and I would sing with Stevie Nicks, nearly always followed by a pause, a lump in our throats, holding back the tears that were a reminder of how true it was of us. We built, like layering bricks and cement, a home out of our love, the only thing sturdy on any given day. Our fights were hurricanes, our love though, indelible.

Of course, we were using anger as a shield to protect us from facing deep hurt and immense fear in the face of scarcity. We'd chase it with tenderness because how else could we face the day? It was a pyrrhic skill that I continue to carry with me. A method of engagement that damaged relationships, certainly, but then again—how easy it's been for me to love so hard, to so stubbornly repair hurt.

It was a terrible way to learn love, but it was better than not knowing love at all. I never doubted that my mom loved me more than anything, and that she would love me profoundly and without condition. There was never one instance when she made me feel like I had to change, not one second when she didn't make it clear that I was the most important thing to her in the world. That unwavering love, though, came with the tumult of unfettered emotions, a restless seed planted in the parched and cracked earth of economic instability.

We were never set up for success.

We loved anyway.

Just not always well.

9.

It's Better, My Sweet
That We Hover Like Bees

The house on the left of ours is a duplex that Dominic rents out to the Danicks, then the Parkes. There is a long driveway that leads to a big yard and eventually a barn. There is a garden on the side of the barn, cordoned off by railroad ties. The tomatoes grow wildly.

In our last summer at the house, Evie asks if I want to play in the yard. Yes, I say, let's go play. I wear bicycle shorts and a blue tee with a floral print. We run, we don't need more than this. We reach the garden. The tomatoes! So green, the stems are coated in white fuzz like goosebumps. The air is hot, but the smell of the leaves is cool—like wind, but emerald.

I'm a tightrope walker, I say, placing one foot, then in front, the other, on the long wooden plank, arms out to either side like a plane. I totter, step and another step, and then. The plank rocks beneath my legs, the top of the wood becomes the side, and the ground below is exposed. I see the black dirt, and then.

I am spinning in knives, but the knives are the stingers of bees, and the sound of buzzing is so loud. I am screaming, Evie is too. I keep trying to run forward, but also flailing them away and so I am dancing dizzy in circles, trying to get back to the house. My arms are not mine. Evie has escaped the few that got her and she watches in horror as my entire body is swarmed. "I'm going to get help!" she screams and runs ahead of me.

I am hysterical. My left arm, swinging, hits a rose bush and a thorn slices my forearm. I see blood, but I can't tell what it's from. I keep running and Mom is screaming my name now, running toward me, ushering me into the house and taking off my clothes, swatting away the insects that are attacking in their glory, but then dying. One by one. Bear the dog chomps the fallen soldiers.

Mom and I are both crying. I am pink and puffy and truly every part of my body is on fire. But the buzzing has stopped. Macaulay Culkin died, I whimper as she holds me, remembering the storyline of *My Girl*, which had come out the year before. She puts me in a blanket and insists through tears, "You're not gonna die, peanut. Let's go to the hospital, you're going to be OK." We get in the van and we drive, both in tears, Mom's hand on mine the whole time.

The doctors give me Benadryl and instead of stitching the open gash on my arm, they suture it with a "butterfly" bandage. Flying insects, see, are both medicine and malady. They check my heart rate, my breathing, my blood pressure. They ask me for details. I try to explain. I don't know how to describe it though, the way that the stings felt like light.

The bees, I think, aren't so different from the lighting bugs. It's just that their deaths come so much easier.

PART 2

AN ALTERNATIVE:
BROOKLYN HEIGHTS
AND COVENTRY ROAD

"It's the price of rootlessness. Motion sickness. The only cure: to keep moving."

—Mr. Lies

"It's good to want things."

—Dinky Bossetti

10.
A Way to Get My Hands Untied

I was in fourth grade when we lost the house in Valley View. But at this point, Mom had worked her way up from the cafeteria in the lighting company to a job in the print shop at the same place, and we were off of welfare.

We moved to Brooklyn Heights, the town adjacent to Valley View, and still in the same school system. We bought a bungalow. I say "we" as though I had anything to do with it, but even at ten years old I felt like Mom's co-pilot, rather than her passenger. We were, as always, in it together.

Brooklyn Heights was less rural than Valley View, but our neighbors were still solidly blue-collar. Unlike in Valley View, though, Brooklyn Heights neighbors complained about the height of the grass Mom didn't have time to mow, or the lack of curtains on our windows. And we lived across the street from a cop, which made us both uncomfortable: my experience with cops was that they did nothing useful the night of my Dad's accident, nothing to protect Rita from Dan, and they took my mom to jail when what I needed was her with me. But I had my sights set on things bigger than rural white-trash living, and even Brooklyn Heights felt like a step in the right direction. It was a little closer to Cleveland, which thrilled me, and we even had a flight of stairs in the house. It felt like a shift to a new chapter—we were both so hopeful, we were both so ready for this to be when things got good again.

———

Mom gives me the entire top floor of the bungalow, which is really just a glorified attic. Half of it is all dusty, unfinished, exposed insulation, but the half where we put my bed has a proper hardwood floor and painted walls. By fourth grade, when we move in, I feel like a teenager. It is no wonder to me that I seemed to behave, in some ways, like I was sixteen when I was only ten. Partly that's because trauma makes you confront the reality of life from which (middle-class, white) children are usually shielded. And partly it's because there were adults in my life who would talk to me, or at least around me, like I was one of them. This would show up in different ways—with my working-class community, it was in swearing, making lewd jokes, and not censoring anything. But with my uncle and my grandparents, it was a pedagogical intervention. Uncle Dana was always saying things I didn't understand, then following up and asking if I knew what he meant. "He's not fiscally conservative enough to sway moderates," he might say, then, "Do you know what 'fiscal' is?" I would shake my head and he'd explain. I was a little street-smart and a little book-smart, but I was also a little lacking in a proper childhood. This combination made me a little weird, but it definitely made me constantly daydream about being a for-real adult.

In the attic bedroom, I have a floor-length mirror we got on sale at TJ Maxx. Cut-out magazine pictures of women I want to look like, and whose energy I long to embody, are taped around the frame. Fiona Apple, with heavy black eyeliner and streaky mascara is on one side, Marilyn Monroe, applying lipstick, is on the other. Drew Barrymore (in a maroon dress and deep lipstick to match, with daisies in her hair) and Liv Tyler (in her *Empire Records* outfit, a short plaid skirt and fuzzy baby-blue sweater that reveals her midriff), join them soon after. I have a Caboodle with Wet n Wild cosmetics from Rite Aid splayed open in front of me. I am ready to put on a face for the day, which I am allowed to do on the weekends. Even Mom, who sets almost no rules, has told me not to wear makeup to school quite yet. I put on a Frank Sinatra CD and try to do a cat-wing on my eyelid with liquid liner. I look in the mirror the way Marilyn looks at the camera. I dance around my room feeling old-fashioned, evoking the energy of my grandmother, who saunters around her home in long gowns and strappy gold sandals. I imagine being at a piano bar in New York City, I imagine how big and glamorous life will be when I am a grown up. I close my eyes and envision the apartment I'll have, the sound of the taxis, the hardwood floors and industrial ceilings I imagine in every NYC brownstone.

I sit on my futon and begin to act as though I am on a date with a man. I do this a lot. As an only child and an aspiring actress, it's not uncommon for me to perform entire plays or scenarios quietly to myself in my bedroom. I write them down too. Sometimes in the form of *ER* fan fiction in which I create a character who is a sex worker who Dr. Carter has to save. But today, I am without a script.

"My play opens on Friday," I say to the imaginary person, crossing my legs toward him. "Will you come see it?" I am learning to be coy.

"Of course," I shift the pitch of my voice several octaves lower.

Suddenly I'm self-conscious in my Marilyn-attire; I want to feel more hot than classy. So I go to the mirror and put several more coats of eyeliner below my eyes, and fasten a black choker at my neck. I don't have a sense of it in any conscious way, but this is when my gender finds its footing, through an exploration and ownership of sexuality that I have been admiring for years. It's a complicated blend of the trashy women of Tinkers Creek and the Old Hollywood chic that my grandmother leaned into effortlessly, along with the languid and aggressive femininity of alternative nineties women. I wasn't exposed to riot grrrl at that point, but its aesthetic had already found its way into the movies and music videos I was drawn to. Dark lipstick, combat boots, control: I am pulled to vintage glamour but I'm more seduced, this afternoon, by grunge.

I walk back to the futon.

"You know," I say, tucking my hair behind my ear, "as a kid I always dreamed of being in New York. And now being here, it's . . . like a dream come true."

I voice my date again: "*You're* a dream come true."

I pretend to kiss this man who I envision as some mix between Josh Hartnett and Noah Wyle, and also, in a flash, Clea Duvall. Suddenly I'm overcome by a pulsing between my legs. I've just begun making myself cum at this point. I mostly use pillows or T-shirts and grind myself against them until the vibration and the release. I learned about the pillow technique from a YA book I got at the library—a story about a girl who leaves home at seventeen and becomes a stripper and makes herself cum on a pillow, and at eleven, I decide that, along with *Catcher in the Rye*, it is my favorite book.

I'm still kissing the air, and now I'm straddling this pretend person. I know I'm in the house alone for another hour so I grab the pillow and unzip my pants. I slide it between my legs and collapse my weight on top of it. I mimic what I see in the movies. I moan quietly, still self-conscious but also eager to perform pleasure. As I cum I can see the poster of the cast of *Friends* above my dresser and I think about the apartment I will have in New York someday and it feels like freedom.

———————

All of my ideas of grown-up life in big cities come from a mix of movies, TV, and Coventry Road. Around the same time that we move to Brooklyn Heights, my uncle takes me to the Centrum, a movie theater he called an "art house" theater. After a few visits, I decide that "art house" must mean movies that nobody's heard of and that are confusing. But also, they are beautiful. I didn't always follow what was going on, but I was mesmerized by the close-ups and the lighting and the music.

We see *Welcome to the Dollhouse* and I am charged with the electricity it takes to make the film reel *click click click*. I am alive with the sound of the popcorn machine and the way every person in the theater looks like what I imagine to be the aesthetic of the East Coast. We stay for the credits. I don't want to leave.

I remember the way the light looked on the sidewalks that night. The flicker of the marquee mixed with a streetlamp. It was a soft yellow-white. Muted but also vivid. It's how I felt most days after that. My brain buzzing with potential—with what my life could, would, should be—but also deeply grounded in the present, in exactly who and where I was. Sometimes presence felt like being trapped, other times I wanted every minute of the days I knew were the foundation for preparing. Preparing for who I would become, just not quite yet.

A white teenager with a mohawk is in front of us. He is watching two Black men with dreadlocks play bongos. A wealthy white woman in flowing linen slides her fingers up and down the chain of a turquoise necklace. I smell what is probably weed but I don't know that yet. I smell garlic from Mongolian Barbeque, the only chain that's managed to make it on the strip. My uncle is talking to my mom and I am taking in everything around us, body humming and mesmerized.

Coventry became a synecdoche for the life I knew I might have someday; Interstate 77 a portal taking me from slow and steady blue-collar chaos into Cleveland through the long strip of deteriorating buildings on Carnegie, then finally to the part of Cleveland Heights that is mansions, parking meters, vintage marquees, and people who talked about big ideas. By sixth grade, I am eager to return to the Centrum as often as possible—if not for a movie, then just anywhere on Coventry, a strip that was busy back then with tattoo parlors, record stores, and organic cafes. In my memory, it is a sepia-toned montage of Nirvana songs and chokers and flannel shirts with cut-off jean shorts and maroon-dyed hair and local coffee shops before Starbucks was a major threat. The sidewalks of Coventry feel like clouds. I am walking on and toward what I want to become, and who I am already becoming.

"Alternative" as an idea fits easily. It makes sense that I am drawn like a calling to the art that wasn't entirely intelligible to "the mainstream." It makes sense that I feel recognized in atemporal narrative structure and off-pitch vocals. It makes sense that I see beauty in what others call trashy: short cut-off shorts, big flannels, combat boots. The general ethos of the nineties that I am being shaped by is rooted in a kind of slacker disposition, and yet these Gen X figures feel to me more like charged warriors in their anti-uniforms and disdain for yuppies. I don't have the ability to unpack the privilege that, for example, refusing to *sell out* one must be afforded, and so instead I find kinship here. I am thirteen when I get a copy of Ani DiFranco's *Little Plastic Castles*, and her spoken word contempt for presidents, and "hum-drum hit songs," and the loss of making records, of events, of people in a room . . . somehow speaks to me. I memorize the entire album and I feel, in my barely teenage mind, disillusioned and angry. And also so romantic about it.

The best part about finding out who you are is the craving. Then, Coventry, or certain CDs, or particular images in magazines felt like a mild addiction. Like I was crawling out of my skin to be wherever I felt more like myself. Hearing the opening bar of "All I Really Want" on *Jagged Little Pill*. Flipping through *Cleveland Scene* at Arabica Coffee House and circling the concerts I want to see (and eventually learning to call them "shows"). It feels so good to want things so desperately, that when you finally get them, it's like water on cottonmouth, like a sigh, or a bed when you're exhausted. It's the sinking deep relief when you know what you love with such certainty that it becomes how you make sense of yourself.

———————

I wasn't the first person to feel that way on Coventry. Although it had been a relatively thriving business district since the early 1900s, it got a reputation for being a Midwest Haight-Ashbury in the sixties, at the height of the Vietnam War, the Civil Rights Movement, the student resistance, and the state violence against it. It helped that it's located within walking distance of residential Cleveland Heights, which has long been a unique example of the sustainability of mixed-class living. It's also the home of two universities: John Carroll and Case Western are both a walk or a bus ride away. And so, like any good subcultural haven, it's been a district that appeals to wide swaths of people. Socialist literati grad students, poets and writers, folks experiencing housing instability, hippies (then later punks), the immigrant workers who sweep the street, the philosophers who made money but still want to live as though they haven't, the local residents who just want a sandwich, and the ones who overlap nearly all those categories—they've all left their breath, their shoe prints, their audible sighs on Coventry Road.

A streetcar ran down the middle of the street until the 1920s, but once that was removed, big open patches of grass created a perfect public space. Artists and musicians and homeless folks would just gather to be outside together. And, for a while, that was OK. Before neoliberal assaults on "third spaces"—not home, not work, but a public space unattached to labor—it was simply, radically, "the common(s)."

To quote Marxist historian David Harvey: "Through their daily activities and struggles, individuals and social groups create the social world of the city and, in doing so, create something common as a framework within which we all can dwell. While this culturally creative common cannot be destroyed through use, it can be degraded and banalized through excessive abuse." The common is utopian at its core, but so rarely can be achieved in practice. Instead, we get glimpses of it. "Temporary autonomous zones" for living how we desire.

Coventry Road in the nineties was a common that materialized culture, but, also, vice versa; the cultural common —the shared set of language and values—materialized Coventry Road. The street became a symbol for something so much larger than concrete or even quirky shops. It was, through the quotidien doings of the motley crew that roamed there, an effigy of *the alternative*. And the public space from which that alternative could breathe, its fertile soil.

"I was a punk rocker," Rob Pryor says to *Cleveland Voices* of his days as a patron of Record Revolution on Coventry, of which he is now a co-owner, "so we hung out on the streets." And when you *want* to hang out on the street, he goes on to explain, you start to spend your days with people who *have* to hang out on the street.

"We had a cat named Benny that we used to go around with, and he was kind of an addict of crack cocaine . . . but he was also like a street prophet!" Pryor is Black. He doesn't mention if Benny is, but a lot of Pryor's punk rock friends and fellow Record Rev patrons were white. I remember Coventry like this: a mix of races and classes and styles. A blend that felt magic and impossible and, with more political consciousness, a version of how it ought to be if only the resources could have been distributed more evenly.

Of course, the freedom Pryor describes—and the way I remember that feeling too—wasn't the case for everyone. Coventry was also the site of the deep repression of artists and anything that could be deemed "obscene." This included a

1959 police raid of the movie theater that showed a screening of *The Lovers*. It included the arrest of d. a. levy and the youth to whom he distributed his poetry. It has included, like every place in America, racism and police brutality, and ultimately shooing all those people "hanging out" in the grass off the lawn and into places where they are forced to buy things.

But in 1995, I'm not aware of any of that. I am just infatuated with the weirdos, the ones who wouldn't make it a day in my rural white-bread school, but who seem here to be thriving.

————————

I begin to ask Mom to take me to Coventry on Saturdays with a friend—Kat or Sami and Abby, sometimes Kendra—and let us walk around by ourselves. It was the alternative culture equivalent of getting dropped off at a mall.

There is a store on the strip that smells like patchouli as soon as you open the door. I can't decide if I like the smell, but it does come to signify what I want to be a part of. There is a pale white woman, behind a counter of crystals and beaded jewelry in a long flowing skirt and a tiny midriff T-shirt. Her hair is short and a little spiky. She has on lipstick so dark purple it is nearly black. A black velvet choker necklace rests tight on her neck. I decide she is one of the most beautiful women I've ever seen.

She catches me staring and I quickly look away.

A few years later, someone will mention "the lesbian witches of Coventry" and I will think of her and I will think it sounds so powerful and perfect and I will think, *Maybe that's what I want to be.*

11.
Come as You Are

I become best friends with Kat the day before kindergarten, back when both our families were relatively normal. We play dolls on the day that the parents are invited to get a preview of what their children will do when school begins. Kat is adorable, with her room-lighting smile and fountain ponytail in the middle of her head. I am still pretty cute myself, with platinum blonde curls and rosy cheeks. Perhaps that's why we are drawn to each other, and when doll playing comes easy, the connection is confirmed. A few months later, my father will get hit by the car. Kat's family, in the nicer part of Brooklyn Heights, will continue to remain stable for years after, and I will envy them, but also, I am invited into it. I get rides with her mom, Lonnie, in the family's BMW; I watch Kat and her older sisters do choreographed dances to "Chevy's Girls," an old *Saturday Night Live* bit from the seventies; her father, Stan, makes us tacos for dinner. But then the girls' Aunt Melanie dies of a drug overdose. Shortly after, Lonnie and Stan will begin to fight and Lonnie will begin to drink and Kat will usher me out of the kitchen when Lonnie's voice is strange and when she is using Hostess mini-muffins as scoops for the margarine bucket, telling us between bites, that we are *such good girls*. I will recognize the heat on Kat's face, I will feel her heart beat the way mine did when I found my mom screaming in the front yard, *Frances, oh, Frances!* And we will say nothing about it, but when we play in her room and turn on Buzzard radio, Nirvana or Crash Test Dummies or the Cranberries will muffle what's unsaid, and the air will be heavier and we will both hold these secrets of our families, together now.

Lonnie and Stan eventually divorce, and although the girls stay with their mom in the beginning, soon they will live mostly with Stan, who moves to a rental on Schaaf Road. This is when we become closer friends with Sami, who lives down the street, and eventually, when we move in with Mom's boyfriend, I will live down the street too.

Sami's family also has secrets. For one, the kind man we know as her father is not her biological father. And her mom is afraid to leave the house. There are also moments inside of Sami's house when she turns red, when Kat and I feel her sped-up heartbeat, the same one we experience when friends witness what we've tried so hard to hide. But we understand it. *We understand,* we tell her with our eyes. Kat and I love her and want to protect her, but there is only so much we can do when rumors spread at school. Thankfully, Sami is pretty and popular in spite of this.

We are an odd mix—by middle school, Kat and I are a little awkward looking, but Sami is considered hot. Kat and I are smart; Sami is too, but her grades don't show it. Kat and I love theater; Sami likes volleyball. We are developing different school friends, but most weekends we are sleeping over at one another's houses. We have inside jokes, we get in fights and make up from them. My mom loves them like daughters. (Years later she will be invited to their weddings, and they will both want pictures of her with them in their wedding dresses. She will love looking at Instagram pictures of the babies they will both have, and she will ask me on the phone, "Did you see Sami's post today? Bri is such a ham!" or, "Did you see Kat's picture of Daisy's birthday? She looks so grown-up!")

Sami, Kat, and I will spend the three summers of middle school together, nearly inseparable. Taking enormously long walks—from Brooklyn Heights to the Cleveland Zoo, with a stop at the psychic and the antique store in Old Brooklyn on the way; three miles to a bus stop so we can take the RTA to Tower City, where we feel both scared and exhilarated; down the street to the new development they are building off Schaff, making up stories about the construction site workers, how maybe one of them could become Sami's boyfriend. We dress similarly—in the sort of flannel we see Claire Danes wear on *My So-Called Life*, each of us with a pair of wide-leg jeans from the Gap, each of us adorned with frosted lip gloss and some piece of jewelry from Claire's. And we will end every day with one of about six movies that we watch on repeat, eating our weight in Kraft macaroni and cheese, Dove Promises, and Pepsi-Cola.

We love all the same songs and albums. We sing along to music our Strathmore friends aren't allowed to listen to. Sami and I in particular seem especially drawn to the hyper-sexual songs. Kat sometimes shakes her head as Sami and I karaoke along with Liz Phair, "Everytime I see your face, I think of things unpure unchaste, I want to fuck you like a dog, I'll take you home and make you like it." Or with Art Alexakis, like he's singing about us, "She dances topless when she's not playing in her band," and, "all you want is just a slow fuck in the afternoon." (Being cash-poor doesn't inherently make you more open to liberated sexuality, but it was also telling, I think, that Sami and I didn't scrunch our noses at the thought of stripping. It was like any other job where you sold your body, which was all of them. I understood this early.)

Actually, we also get jobs together. None of our Strathmore friends have to work, but at twelve, the three of us devise ways to make money. Serving food at rich people's parties, Sami and I flipping burgers at Wendy's, Kat making coffee at Starbucks. We crammed in Kat's Aunt Holly's pickup truck and helped her haul soil and plant flowers during her short-lived attempt at a landscaping business where she paid her workers (us) primarily in McDonald's lunches and ELO sing-alongs. And then after a day of labor, we'd stay together through the evening too. "What do you want to watch tonight?" one of us might ask as our shifts were ending, knowing there was not a question about whether or not we'd be gathering at Stan's house for a sleepover. Of course we were.

(When you think about it, really sit with it, the love built between young girls will knock the wind out of you.)

We will rarely talk about the state of our lives in any big-picture way. We have a ferocious tenacity for staying present. There are pockets of these days when we are allowed to be just kids, and we cling to it.

12.
. . . Even When I Was Twelve

I am eleven, in sixth grade, and we are in the car driving Kat home from Odyssey of the Mind (OM) practice, a creative performance group that Mom coaches, when Mom announces that she has something to tell me.

Before I tell you what she told me, I have to tell you about my mother's car. My mother's cars. We would drive them until they died, and they'd become statues in the yard or driveway. Yard as burial ground—another marker of white trash. It embarrasses me. It's even worse that both the dead and living cars become storage units. Mostly for Mom's newspapers, the extras she doesn't end up delivering. The bright orange plastic bags that serve as Roxy's poop bags and Mom's makeup bag and sometimes the bags I'll use to bring my lunch to school. The cars are filled with Drug Mart bags too, holding things that were on sale that we don't really need, but just in case we do, Mom wants to buy them when they're cheaper: off-season holiday candy—Peeps in May, red and green M&M's in January. The car that works will hold OM props, things from work Mom has printed for me— school papers, pictures of actors I like, pictures of actors *she* likes (mainly, in this era, Spike from *Buffy*). And of course, fast food wrappers. Bags from Wendy's and Burger King, and even when we stopped eating fast food, Mom would still buy a super size unsweetened iced tea from McDonald's nearly every day. The old cups would live in the car after she'd gallivant around work and our family gatherings with them. "Jolie, don't you want a glass for that?" Nana or Ammie would ask, more like a plea. "No. I like my cup," Mom would say, straw in her mouth.

Our cars were messy is what I'm trying to say. And I hated it and swore I'd never have a messy car, but then when I'm thirty and working two jobs and living alone and coping with symptoms of C-PTSD and rushing always everywhere, I begin to notice how easy it is to *accumulate,* and I see a glimpse of Mom's car in the maroon station wagon I drive in Boston. I will laugh so hard I cry the day I notice this.

And this day in the car, Kat probably had to move trash out of the way to make space, and she is sitting amidst it when Mom says:

"Peanut," she begins, and I can tell she is nervous. "I ran into an old boyfriend from high school at Drug Mart. We have been talking and I'm going to start seeing him."

I glance back at Kat, whose parents had divorced and had both started dating other people. She gives me a face that doesn't tell me how I should feel but lets me know, in her way, that she'll be there for me through this.

I run through the narratives of how I'm supposed to react. I think of movies and television shows in which children are angry at men replacing their fathers. But I barely remember what it's like to have a father. So I decide I will be happy for her.

"OK, Mom," I say. "What's his name?"

———————

Ron is awkward and uncomfortable to be around right away. He talks like he has rocks in his mouth and he's committed to maintaining a dated haircut from the seventies, with a side part and long sideburns. He's obsessed with Elvis. He works in some kind of factory which means he wears a light blue shirt with his name sewn on a patch on the pocket. He tries to be kind, but I'm instantly deep in my gut creeped out by him, and so I am generally not very receptive to his efforts at conversation.

Mom and Ron go from dating to us moving in with him in what seems like just a few short months, and by the end of sixth grade, we pretty much live there full-time. The good news is that he lives right next door to Sami and right down the street from Kat. Mom uses this as a selling point. Keith will still stay at the Brooklyn Heights house around the corner. I feel comforted that it will still be there if I need it, but we will almost never go back.

Ron's house is bigger than any house I've ever lived in, but it's also in terrible shape. Like his hair, the decor is from the seventies and it seems like no one has cleaned it in over a decade. It has a weird smell. There are bright orange mushrooms painted on ceramic pots that line nearly every shelf. The floors are a mix of torn-up carpet and unfinished linoleum. I am given a bedroom that belonged to his daughter, who now lives with his ex-wife. It still has her toys in it—a dollhouse, some Barbies. The walls are a light seafoam, like the color of a Florida nursing home. I am unhappy there and express it, usually by saying as little as possible to Ron.

In the beginning, Mom seems happy-ish. I don't remember her and Ron acting super in love. But she seems glad to have a partner again.

My memories in the house are almost entirely bad. My memories of his car are absolutely entirely bad. He would corner me, a lot—in bedrooms, against walls, locking the car doors—so we could "talk." So he could explain why I should like him more. These conversations would almost always begin with him as a gentle victim who was just trying to make things better for his girlfriend and her daughter, but they would often end with me being an "ungrateful bitch."

These encounters made me even more stubborn. I dug my heels in the fucking ground. I wasn't budging on my conviction that he was no good for my mom, no good for me. She deserved better and I wasn't going to act happy that we were stuck with him.

He made all my friends uncomfortable too. We would have OM meetings at the house, sometimes sleepovers, and he'd always say something inappropriate. One night, Mom let us watch *Boogie Nights,* knowing full well we were really only interested in the Mark Wahlberg penis shot. It was a memorably hilarious night—at one point Megan decided we should draw pictures of the penis, and so we did, laughing so hard we could barely breathe.

Ron found the pictures the next morning, and in front of all of us, said, "Looks like mine."

My friends looked mortified and also scared.

I hated him.

———————

In the worst period of time at Ron's, when fights between him and me and him and Mom and me and Mom were daily, usually multiple times a day, a boy in my eighth-grade class said he saw him walking around the halls at school. I felt simultaneously cold and hot with fear; sweat and shivers both stabbing my skin at once. I was filled with dread; he had no reason to be at my school, and now school felt like a possible place to be cornered, to be confronted, being ordered to explain myself.

The next day in English class, Mark Kimble, my best guy friend, returned from the bathroom and approached Mr. Boston in an uncomfortable whisper. I noticed him looking over at me as he spoke, and then Mr. Boston looked my way too, mouth open. I remember that I was wearing a teal sweater that I had gotten in the sale bin at Express and I started to sweat through it.

"All right," Mr. Boston bellowed the way he did, "Keep doing your work. Raechel come with me." He paused. "Mark, you too."

We walked a short silent walk to the middle school principal's office down the hall. Mr. Boston told the secretary he needed to speak to Mr. Kenny. I still had no idea what was going on. Mark and I sat in the chairs reserved for scolded students. "Mark," Mr. Boston said, exasperated. "Tell her."

Mark looked nervous. "There was writing in the boys' bathroom," he said. "About you."

My heart sped up. I felt nauseous. I knew it was Ron.

"What did it say?"

A pause.

"Mark, please tell me," I pleaded, in tears.

"Big lips, small tits, for a good time call Raechel at 216-222-1334."

The only boys who knew my phone number—which was Ron's phone number—were Mark and Lars. I guess it could have been Lars, who I "dated" briefly in sixth grade, but I had no reason to believe he'd write that. It had to have been Ron.

My head fell in my hands. Mark awkwardly placed a hand on my shoulder. Then he did the best thing possible: "I'm gonna go get Kat and Sami."

Kat and Sami comforted me in the office. I don't remember talking to the principal. I remember Madame, my French teacher, coming in. I didn't want to tell her the details, but she tried to soothe me anyway. "Oh Joelle, *ma chere*," she cooed the name I'd chosen for French class. Sami hugged me. Kat sat next to me, quietly sharing my anger, sharing my fear. Kat had a calm, stoic empathy that you didn't recognize until you were in it, pummeled by her intense compassion. She's a real Virgo in that way.

"They'll paint over it," Mr. Boston announced, not making eye contact as he left the office.

Sami, Kat, and I sat together a little longer: three girls from broken homes who understood that sometimes you can't rely on the grown-ups. They both had biological sisters, but they may as well have been mine. They were, in our adventures and our understanding of the kind of pain you had to keep quiet, my family.

13.
So Much for the Afterglow

I begin to notice my hair falling out in two spots on the back of my head—doctors tell me and Mom it's alopecia, which is often caused by stress. I wear my hair in a ponytail every day to try to hide the bald spots. When I'm at home, I stroke the spots tearfully, twirling the long strands that surround them like I did as a child, then yanking out the new hair growth. I don't understand why I do this, but for at least a year it feels so comforting, and impossible to stop.

The deep-breath problem amplifies around now too. For as long as I can remember, after the accident, there would be days I couldn't take a deep breath. And I would be overcome with an urgent need to take one—"But I can't get it, Momma." Mom told me she had the same thing: "I have the same thing, peanut! Just try not to think about it, it'll come back." When we were finally able to catch it, usually it was audible. Our home was a cacophony of perceptible sighs, and we'd recognize the other's victory when we heard it.

Trauma is an incoherent language of the body.

Trips to Coventry got me through this time period, as did movies and delusional obsessions with actors who I was convinced I could marry. I learned to make myself throw up, disappearing my finger down my throat every chance I could. I went to Kat's house; I listened to music.

When Kat's sister Ellen starts driving, we get rides to school in the used maroon Oldsmobile she buys with her barista money. Ellen is an appropriately sullen teen; I admire her a lot. She wears wing-tip cat eyeliner every single day. Sometimes, when she leaves her bedroom door open, I'll watch her apply it. I study how she tilts her head up, how she finds a way to do something meticulous with her eyes half-closed. I gape: *What a miraculous and stunning skill.*

And from her friends at Arabica, Ellen learns about indie and punk music, which she plays on mixtapes in the car. I feel really cool and reflective in the early morning drives to school. I become obsessed with a song called "No Love" by the Get Up Kids. Kat and Abby are too. We ask Ellen to play that part of the tape every morning.

The Get Up Kids sound nothing like I've ever heard, not even on 107.9 The End, the alternative music station that Kat and I listened to religiously. There is something deeply gritty about this song playing from a cassette tape in an old car. If Coventry was a key to a new life, this song felt like permission to actually come inside. It was a sound that made me close my eyes, breathe heavy, a sound that made me feel like I was floating underwater. I felt completely shaken.

When we were allowed to go on the computers at school, I would google the band's name. When we got a computer at home, I would search their name in AOL profiles, then write down the names of the bands people listed alongside them. I was desperate on this scavenger hunt for what I was learning was considered punk or emo, sometimes ska. Feverishly jotting down bands and imagining what they sounded like. Ordering CDs from the library, putting the ones I couldn't live without on the wish list my grandmother always requested around my birthday. Instead of boys' names, I scrawled lyrics on the paper bags we turned into textbook covers. I sang them in my head during the classes I found dull. Every new band felt like a precipice. To what I didn't know yet, but something was coming.

———

Mom, I think, was eager to compensate for my anger about living with Ron, and she continued to go above and beyond parental duties—coaching our nerdy creative performance group, taking us to Coventry or the mall whenever we asked, taking us on yearly "vacations," which meant an overnight anywhere we could get on a tank of gas (Pittsburgh, Cincinnati, Detroit), and taking us to concerts. Sometimes during this period she could afford a ticket for herself. Other times she'd stand outside the fence at Nautica after asking security to please keep an eye on us: me, Sami and Kat, and sometimes Abby. We were all still friends with the girls in Strathmore, but a lot of the stuff we did wasn't OK with the middle-class parents. Kat's parents, Sami's parents, and my mom all had a lower bar for what was and wasn't acceptable for preteens.

Mom didn't bat an eye about spending so much of her time carting us around. I remember how excited she was at our excitement about seeing a show. We hooked up a Discman to the car with a cassette jack, and we blasted No Doubt, Alanis Morrissette, Ben Folds Five, Everclear, Third Eye Blind, Our Lady Peace, Liz Phair, Fiona Apple. Later we moved on to Reel Big Fish, New Found Glory, MxPx, the Get Up Kids, Saves the Day (and so on). We could hardly stand the anticipation that we were going to hear the same songs live. Mom just seemed happy she could help make it happen.

In the spring of eighth grade, she spent an entire day and night tracking the whereabouts of the DJs on 107.9, on the last day that they were a station. Listeners had just gotten news that Clear Channel would be buying them out and changing the format. We were devastated. Where else would I tune in to hear Green Day, Garbage, or Hole? Soul Coughing or Poe? On the last days of the station, the DJs played "It's the End of the World as We Know It (And I Feel Fine)" by R.E.M. on a loop.

Mom picked us up from school and said she heard that Howie Green, Sue, and Number One Son, our favorite of the DJs, were all at the station downtown. She'd drive us there. We listened to R.E.M. on the drive, not getting tired of singing between tears that the world was ending. We were earnest twelve- and thirteen-year-olds, and Mom not only indulged, but affirmed our obsessions. She didn't say, "It's just a radio station," she said, "Oh, I know I know I know, what will we do without this music?!" She wasn't embarrassed to herd us to the station, to approach the DJs to say, "You meant everything to these girls, and we'll miss you."

Mom believed us. She didn't question us. In her deeply empathetic bones, she felt everything with us. It's why when Clarissa, one of my friends on the OM team, decided to start having sex before the rest of us, she asked Mom to take her to Planned Parenthood. And Mom did, without judgment or question. I didn't really drink at all until college, but Mom always made sure I knew that if I did, she'd be there to drive me home.

In so many ways, she did everything right. In nearly all of the ways, she was doing beyond well for a lower-income single mother.

And yet.

14.

[...]

The second time someone held me down on a bed with force, I was twenty-two and my body sank gloriously with release. His hand held my neck softly at first, and then—after eye contact and my head nodding desperately in approval and for more—harder. I remember making a connection, in the pocket of a second, of all the ways pain had entered my body during what we broadly define as sex, or sex-like, or sex-adjacent: the cramp in my wrist when I'd ride my fingers alone; the high I got after one of my college boyfriends bit my inner thigh so hard it left bruises; the weight of my mom's boyfriend on top of my small body. I was scared by this mix of these experiences I enjoyed, and the one that made me terrified for my life.

After college, I sought more and more extreme versions of domination. Restraints, slapping, choking, degradation. And of course I have asked myself if these predilections are evidence of being a sick victim, or if in fact, they are a way to take back power. I think it's the latter, but I can't know for sure about the pathology of the broken, about what is and isn't a "healthy" coping mechanism. At a certain point I decided that even if it was a result of trauma, I wanted it anyway. With people I trusted, at least, I wanted to set the ground rules for being treated like I had absolutely no control. ("In receiving consensual pain," says dominant rope bondage practitioner Daemonu X, "it is essential to trust and be trusted, which is perhaps the most intimate of all.")

And so anyway, that was the second time. The first time, I was just scared. There was nothing in my bones or blood or skin that wanted what was happening. I whimpered. I begged for him to please leave, to remove his body from my body. To take the weight away, *please please please leave.*

It started in a doorway. The doorway of the bedroom I was given in his house when it was clear we'd be staying there more often than we'd stay at the bungalow that we'd declare bankruptcy on shortly after moving in. I was on the bed, opening my journal, which was a standard, nearly daily practice. But this time, when I opened the book, loose pages fell out. I panicked. I had not put anything in the journal, what was this? I unfolded what I saw was a Xerox copy. It was a duplicate of my last few journal entries. The ones where I'd been writing about making myself throw up my food. About wanting to be thinner. About hating my body. About my routine of drawing a bath and pressing play on the Discman from which I'd blast the Sarah McLachlan CD so loud that you could hear it through headphones, so that the combination of that noise would drown out the sound of me retching. And how I'd lock the door even though my mom made me promise I'd never do that in the shower or the bath, because if I slipped, she needed to be able to open the door. And how I had kept that promise for my whole life until now, but I just couldn't risk her catching me throw up, and also, I wrote, *because of Ron.*

My heart rate was out of control. In that instant, Ron appeared in the doorway.

"I did this to help you," he said, or something along those lines. Forgive me for not remembering it all verbatim.

"You shouldn't do this to yourself," he slurred. "You're beautiful."

I protested. How could you do this? This is my private journal.

He got closer and closer and closer and closer and closer and I don't know how I knew what was going to happen was going to happen, but I did. As soon as I saw him standing there. As soon as I realized that his shark eyes had been as predatory as I imagined.

I think I was sitting. I must've been. In swishy pants (that's what I called them, these ugly old track pants) and a powder-blue sweatshirt, braces, my hair in a bun. I was as awkward and covered up as one can be at thirteen. Swishy pants and a powder-blue sweatshirt that the bands of my braces matched.

Somehow, then, I was on my back. And he was heavy on top. His own blue shirt with his name tag. *Ron.* In stitched cursive. He had just come from work.

"I would love to go down on you," he said between my tears, my pleading.

Iwouldlovetogodownonyou.Iwouldlovetogodownonyou. I wouldloveto. Godownonyou. I wouldlovetogodownon you. Iwouldlovetogodownonyou.

I didn't know what it meant but I knew. I thought of the Alanis Morrissette lyric, *Would she go down on you in a theater?* I loved that album, but still never really understood what the act was that she was describing. But I knew, of course, that it was something I didn't want from Ron.

I cried, I whimpered, I begged him to please please please leave. His weight got heavier.

And then . . . he started to cry too. Nothing else was going to happen, I could tell. He started apologizing, still heavy on top of me.

I'm sorry, he said.

He was surely broken too.

He left the room eventually. I don't remember how long he held me down on that bed, I don't remember the color of the comforter or the sheets if maybe I didn't even have a comforter. I don't remember that, but I do remember the weight of him and those eight words.

But I pretended I didn't. I announced to Ron that I would be telling my mom what happened, checking to see if he would maybe kill me, or force me on the bed again, and when he didn't, when he was defeated and he nodded, I took my thirteen-year-old indignation and I readied myself for when Mom would return home.

She ended up calling first, from a pay phone at an outlet mall where she had been on a group bus outing doing some discount Christmas shopping. I began to tell her what happened, but I pretended that I didn't know the words. I sat with her on the phone in their bedroom and said, "You need to come home." I double-checked with Ron, who was just standing there, to see if he'd maybe pull out a gun or choke me to death, and when he still didn't, I said, "Ron told me he wanted to lay me." I cannot recall how much, if anything, more I shared.

Getting laid was a term I knew. It was a sex term a thirteen-year-old knew. I didn't know "going down" and so I changed it to this.

Mom was silent and my heart was about to explode out of my chest with Ron standing in the room, and he actually had the audacity to say, "Well, that's not what I said."

Mom's silence turned to panic. I don't remember her words. I guess it was something about if I was OK, if I was safe, that she would be home soon. *Peanut, peanut, peanut . . . .* Her nickname for me.

───────────────

We stayed weeks, possibly months, after the incident. I don't remember how long. I am angry now that it was even a day. That I slept there that night. We tried to go to a family counselor. Mom stormed out of the session, I don't remember why. We stayed. I understand why, and also I don't. I understand that Mom didn't know where we would live if not with Ron, how we would afford things without his help. I understand that this was the first and only person she'd dated since my dad's accident and that she believed she'd never find anyone else to date again. I understand her fear. How this could have felt like it was actually best for us to work through this mistake so at least I'd have a roof over my head. I understand that it probably felt like our options were Ron's two-story house or a car full of trash. I need you to understand how easy it is to believe she makes all her decisions out of love for me, because it's true: she does. Even this.

At the time, I wasn't capable of being angry at her for staying. That came nearly twenty years later, after a C-PTSD diagnosis revealed I hadn't actually dealt with the trauma of that incident. But at the time, I just tried to get through the days. Besides, if I was mad at Mom, who else would I have?

15.
Momma

I hear stories about Mom from her, from Ammie, from Aunty Bun when she's in town, and some stick with me more than others. Like the time she got sent home from school for sewing an upside-down American flag to the back pocket of her skirt in protest of the Vietnam War. Or the time she painted the inside of the elevator at school all black (I'm not sure what for). How, when she was very little, she used to say, "Oh my stars!" and if Ammie or Gramps asked, "What are we gonna do with you?!" she'd respond, "Keep me and love me and throw me in Dover Lake!"

And of course the stories of John. When Mom talks about John, she is wistful. Her eyes move up and out, searching, I think, for the warmth of the memory of him. John was her soulmate, she's said in so many words, and sometimes in those exact words. He was the brother of Mom's friend Mary, who I grew up calling Aunt Mary. Sometimes John would come up in conversation, but not often. I saw his picture a few times, in a box in the basement. He was wearing a military uniform.

I grew up knowing war was bad but that John, Mom's veteran addict soulmate, was very good. When she talked about him she was lighter. When she talked about him she was who she could have been—a girl in love, a girl with dreams.

Mom explains that although she was critical of the military, it did seem like a good way out. "I thought I was going to join too," she told me, "But John called me from boot camp and said it was terrible and that I'd never make it."

She didn't have to say that John wasn't being mean or critical of her. I knew from her stories and the tone her voice took that John was kind. He just wanted to protect her.

John ultimately "drank himself to death." That's how Mom puts it.

He was with someone else at the time, and Mom was married to Daddy, but she was still shattered by the loss of him.

And then just two years later, she loses her husband, in a different way, but still, another love is gone.

I can mostly barely imagine what this must feel like. It's too painful to let myself consider the impact of these losses on her heart. In my adult life, I have had a handful of relationships whose endings legitimately shattered me. I have hardly been able to breathe after walking out of apartments for the last time. And these people are still alive. But to consider the death of this kind of love. Or the slamming of this kind of love with a booze-stained car that takes memories and understanding away. I cannot, I cannot, I cannot fathom the despair of it.

Many days I feel guilty for not living in the same city as her. Every day I want to find ways to remind her that I'm not going anywhere—in the larger sense, I mean—and that, more importantly, she doesn't deserve to lose love. That she is not the reason for loss. That in fact, if there was any justice in the world, she'd have the kindest love and the most steadfast love. A love that wouldn't dream of abandoning her.

Specifically, she'd have Willie Nelson, who she's more or less described as her dream man. Or at least the Ohio-equivalent of Willie Nelson, who wouldn't be as rich, but would hopefully have enough to give her a little luxury. She likes the long-gray-haired hippies, she likes cowboy boots and motorcycles, she likes people who believe in peace and equality. And although she never says it out loud, I know she'd like to be taken care of. She deserves it. (There is not enough room in this book to tell you how much she deserves it.)

I've lived hundreds of miles from her since I left for college, and so instead of being able to hug her and bring her soup when she's sick, we text as promises that we're each still here. Every single night we tell one another when we are home, report that we are safe, nearly beg that the other sleeps well and is healthy and happy. Of course, we say *I love you*. If I don't hear from her one night, I am convinced she is dead, usually—my brain envisions—in a car. In actuality, she is just asleep or the phone is out of battery. The next morning, after seeing my panicked texts, she will respond, "Sorry, peanut! I was [asleep/charging the phone]."

Sometimes I will check the local Cleveland news and read about any traffic accident that has happened since I last received a text.

Mom is only slightly less panicky when I forget to text. She knows she can text Logan. She knows that Logan would call her if anything happened. I have someone who looks out for me.

We do not say "goodbye" at the end of a phone call. It started as a bit of an homage to my Gramps, who never said anything when he hung up. When he was done with the conversation, you might get an, "OK," then *click*. But then Mom and I started getting superstitious about it. "Goodbye" is so final. "Goodbye" could mean a last time (and in fact, the last voice mail I got from my Gramps before he died, he *did* say goodbye). So it's "goodnight" we say on the phone, even at 1p.m. Once, we accidentally said, "OK, bye" and I hung up with a panic realizing what we'd done—a second later Mom texted, "Goodnight."

"Goodnight," I typed back at three in the afternoon. Never goodbye. Not until we absolutely have to.

When I am twenty-four, I ask my ex-girlfriend to cut open the side of my ankle and stain it with ink with the letters M-O-M on a banner over a heart. A classic flash tattoo to honor this human who deserves so much better than what life has handed her.

The tattoo process hurts as always, but this time I want it to. In honor, in homage, in some attempt at reparations for her labor—my birth, her jobs, the emotional toll of caring for me and Daddy and her dying parents and all the poor people we kept in our home and, and, and.

"How you doing?" Alice asks, lifting the needle gun and wiping my blood with a paper towel.

"Bad," I say, grimacing at the sting. "Keep going."

Mom always does.

16.
I Clicked My Heels Three Times
Just Like You Said

I remember the night we finally flee like a shattered mirror. Shards and screams and a wooden side table flying in the air toward Mom's face and hitting the wall beside her. Screams and yells, the way Ron spat out words, shark eyes. The night outside the door being dark. The police lights. The quiet car ride on the way to my grandparents' house. (But was it quiet or is the sound just off? It's not as much fuzzy as it is in pieces, some parts dark or muted.) I don't remember what we said to my grandparents, if anything. I remember mostly a week into staying there. Sharing the guest room with Mom. Staying up late on the WebTV in the kitchen, filling out surveys and emailing my crushes, tucking the trauma away like it didn't happen. Knowing I couldn't talk about it with anyone. Knowing I couldn't say what was happening: *Ron put his whole weight on top of me in a bed and we stayed a few months after that anyway but finally we left and now we live with my grandmother and we share a twin bed and it creaks and I am only thirteen years old and so I'd rather think about how I have a crush on Jim McCuthers who is normal and lives in Strathmore, so if I tell anyone anything it'll be Kat and Sami who will understand, and I will go to sleep and wake up and I will keep living as though this is all completely fine.*

So instead I say, "Mom and Ron finally broke up, we're staying at Ammie's for a bit."

The guest room where Mom and I sleep at my grandmother's is tiny. And it's full of antique furniture: the bed, the vanity with my great-grandmother's hand mirror and old brush and vintage perfume holders, a desk in the corner. There is not much space to move about. I have a pile of my clothes on a chair. Mom keeps hers in a laundry basket.

We sleep in the same twin bed. And every morning at 3:30 a.m., Mom gets out of bed, trying to be as quiet as possible, to get ready for her newspaper route. She'd use the light in the hallway to find her clothes so that she didn't actually turn on a light in the bedroom. I woke up nearly every morning anyway. "Go back to sleep, peanut," she'd whisper. "Love you, Momma, be safe," I'd murmur and close my eyes again.

When I eventually got up for the day, Ammie would prepare my breakfast—a small bowl of Blueberry Morning cereal with skim milk. Daddad would leave out the comics section of the newspaper in front of the bowl. He'd sit next to me and read his section of the paper and I'd read mine, skipping through the comics, straight to the horoscopes. Then, when I was ready, he'd drive me to school in the Oldsmobile. We'd listen to the old-timey AM radio station playing songs I imagine he'd heard in clubs during his time in the war. We'd rarely talk. He was a quiet and loving and generous man. It's so clear to me how badly they wanted to make me feel taken care of.

They're both gone now, but I hope they know that they succeeded.

17.
"Open hearth furnaces light up the sky..."

Cuyahoga Heights High, where I went to school, has a clear view of the notorious Cleveland smoke stacks, which are a story of course, every time you look at them, of how we do things in the Rust Belt: beams from mens' hands and flames borne of grit; the steel poles even Allen Ginsberg romanticized; a sign that our city wasn't dead—it was a volcano. You can see them from all sides—from Parma, Lakewood, Shaker Heights, from a boat on Lake Erie. On a cloudless night, the flames are truly breathtaking, and when the sky is black, the smoke they cough along with them becomes invisible. They are majestic. They are hard work and industry. They are what makes Cleveland, Cleveland. Right?

My grandfather worked at LTV when they were the ones in charge of the smoke, and when we pass them together, he feels something different. I learn the word "layoff." He is so quiet.

On the other side of my school, there is a sewage plant. Some of the kids who live on East Seventy-first Street get made fun of for living so close to it, but then Justina's stepmom dies of cancer, and Maddie says she heard it was because of the toxic waste, and we all look at Nate whose dad works at the plant. "This school should not be so close to that place," I overhear a teacher complain. We all wonder if we will get cancer like Justina's stepmom.

The street Jackie lives on, just a mile away from Tinkers Creek, is adjacent to a landfill that is rumored to possess toxins that one reporter described as, "the kind of stuff that makes Agent Orange seem like Sierra Mist."

And of course, I know you've heard: once, our river caught on fire.

Still though, in college, after becoming enamored with the labor movement, I visit home with pride. I gaze at the smokestacks and think, *look at this city built by workers' hands!*

Look at the smoke, the labor, the smoke, the river, the waste in Jackie's backyard. What did Justina's stepmom breathe? Does Nate's dad glow in the dark?

But look! Look at this city, built by workers' hands. Even the water, built by workers' hands. A life, a body, for every mile.

18.
1999

We are finally free. Free from Ron, free from sharing an antique bed in a tiny guest room. It is just Mom and me again. The two of us, a team. We find an apartment in a building on the edge of Brooklyn Heights that is technically Cleveland. The rent is more affordable there, and we plan to stay there a year while we figure out if we can manage the mortgage on the Brooklyn Heights bungalow where Keith is still staying. We know it's a risk to move out of the three villages that comprise the school I attend, but we hope, because Daddy still lives in Valley View, that I'll still be able to attend. We decide to ask for forgiveness rather than permission. We cross our fingers and hold our breath; a state that so many poor folks occupy daily. *When will we be caught for trying to survive in a system that offers us no other ways to exist besides cheating it?*

The apartment building is really a house-turned-duplex, and the outside looks kind of like a big red barn. My bedroom doesn't have a door, but I love it. I paint the walls midnight blue and hang up black-and-white pictures from magazines, mostly perfume ads of waify white women staring into the camera while waify white men look at them. I rent CDs from the library and record them onto cassette tapes. I begin to identify with love songs in a very real way. At this point I have gone through my first real heartbreak. And by winter of ninth grade, I am falling in love with a boy named Nico who is two years older than me. He is one of the only "alternative" boys at school. There are only about ten goths, five skaters, and a handful of other people who listen to non-mainstream music and who don't shop at Abercrombie or wear athletic gear. So, to me, Nico is a real catch. He has blue hair, he snowboards, he listens to Tool, and I'll take it.

I learn to flirt. I borrow from the movies, I tap into what feels like a voice from my gut telling me how to behave. I dye my hair box-maroon red and cut my bangs like the ones Gwen Stefani has on the cover of *Return to Saturn*. I buy a hot pink tank top from Hot Topic that I feel truly incredible in. I don't wear a bra with it, which would normally make me feel younger, but I like the way the silk fabric feels against my nipples. I buy Wet n Wild lip gloss in a color that matches the tank top nearly exactly. I am still insecure and still in the throes of bulimia and body hatred, but I also feel something more primal, like a body whisper from femme ancestors—or maybe it's just my grandmother telling me that I am beautiful after all.

When I am with Nico, my body responds with the right hip movements, the right sounds. He is only sixteen, so he does what he's heard from other boys. All we do is make out—aggressively make out—and rub our pelvises together above our clothes. It feels intense. And when he breaks up with me three months later, I am shattered. He cries in the car. (I am still, to this day, grateful to know the tenderness that existed in this sixteen-year-old boy. That the root of these boys is not toxic masculinity, but rather a limited number of places where they can be free—to feel, to be vulnerable, to say this hurts and I'm sorry.)

I grieve heavily. I play Fiona Apple's newest album on repeat. I actually save money to buy this one, not just get it from the library. I journal in my bedroom, leaning against the midnight blue wall, singing along to "Love Ridden" and dripping bulging tears onto the pages. I feel the weight of this loss like boulders have been sewn into the muscles of my chest. And at the same time, I feel an indulgent pleasure in this whole process. I'd never tell anyone, but there is something glorious to me at fourteen, feeling so heartbroken. I am relishing my ability to understand what Fiona is singing, I am smug in my new ability to connect with the characters in films who grieve their beloved. I am, in the midst of the pain, dreaming of how many more loves I will have and how terrible and perfect it will be to lose them too.

19.
Ammie

It's true my grandmother told me I was beautiful. It was hard to believe her, such a vision herself, and I, so round and insecure, felt like a bit of a baby monster in comparison. Ammie—Lois, Mom's mom—was elegant. There is no better word for her. When we watch old musicals together and see Audrey Hepburn or Hedy Lamarr or Judy Garland, I am struck by their glamour, but also by how much they remind me of Ammie. Or Ammie reminds me of them. I will glance from the television screen to Ammie on the couch and be mesmerized by how easy and banal she makes it all look. These actresses had makeup teams and camera lights, but Ammie just has her discount dresses and an absolute air.

In the evening, after a day of teaching two fitness classes to senior women and then tending to the house or reading, she would shower and put on her "clean-up clothes." Clean-up clothes were long dresses, sometimes near gown-like, or silky jumpsuits, or gold lamé palazzo pants and drapey camisoles. And nearly always, a pair of gold shoes—heels when I was younger, but as she got older, gold slippers. (I would go on to get a pair of "house heels" of my own, and they would be, like Ammie's, metallic gold). Ammie would emerge from the upstairs bathroom with enough presence for a red carpet event. And somehow there was no pretension, no vanity, no expectation of awe. Instead, Ammie was being the truest version of herself. One could certainly call her confident, but more than that, she was comfortable, deeply comfortable in her skin, and what it opened up for her was the ability to spend every ounce of her energy loving her family and her friends so big you didn't know what hit you. Ammie had herself figured out and she liked the result of it, and with that settled, it gave her so much space to love, love, love, and then love some more. It was almost confusing that someone with so much poise could give such warm hugs, offer such gentle words.

In her clean-up clothes, Ammie will cook fancy dinners. She is a Julia Child devotee in her desire to have upscale, restaurant-quality dinners more affordably at home. She will make chicken divan, and cheese souffles, and sometimes even lobster. She will have a glass of white wine poured, a cigarette in hand, and she will stir. She never wears oven mitts and when she inevitably burns herself on a pan, she'll barely flinch. She is tough—even while warm and graceful. If a splash of sauce spills on the counter, she's more inclined to wipe it away with her fingers than deal with a rag. No time for rags. Once her fingers are rinsed, she'll pick up her wine and keep cooking.

Lois had loves before Daddad, and also before Gramps. In Amherst, Ohio, when Ammie was a teenager, an only child like me, living with her tender mother, Lydia, and her bigoted father, Clayton, she was in love with Chuck. He would visit her at the town store where she worked, they would talk about getting married. They didn't, but Ammie talks about him, and when she does, you can tell she loves him still. She beams, her smile so big when she says his name.

(I will love hearing about who Mom and Ammie still love anyway, years later, even while loving someone else. It will be a model for me. To remember how endings are so gray. To know that the heart, the more it loves, just gets bigger. Rather than only having the capacity for one story at a time, the heart is as expansive as a tome.)

Gramps doesn't bring a smile to her face. When they were married, he was a drunk and he slept around. Instead, Ammie will say vague things like, "I don't know how your Nana got him sober, but good for her." This will be delivered quietly and testily. When she talks about Gramps, my grandmother is not just my grandmother but also a woman scorned. A beautiful woman scorned.

When Ammie poses for pictures, she will sometimes show us her huge and radiant smile, but other times she'll look toward the camera the way I do today for selfies. Mouth a little pouty, staring directly into the camera with a look she knows could bring men to their knees. I see pictures of her like this mostly from before I was born but even into her 60s those looks will sometimes still emerge. I will pick up on this very early, and when I am five, she does a photo shoot with me on our routine Friday afternoon visit, and I pose like her. At one point I am stretched out on her bay windowsill like a swimsuit model, resting my head in my hand, propped up on my elbow. Ammie will snap the photo with a laugh and say, "Where did you learn to pose like that?!" Ammie, from you, of course.

Ammie will slow down as she ages, but just a bit. This will show up in fewer gowns, in more sensitivity to noise, more takeout. But it is when Daddad dies that she will first appear old. Her mind begins to go almost exactly at that time. She has been terrified of ending up like her mother, my great-grandmother, who I knew primarily with dementia in a nursing home. We will be glad to never have to send Ammie to a nursing home, but for a year, Mom will take care of her as her brain deteriorates, and she will live the last six months of her life barely eating, resting on a couch, and half-watching television. It will break our hearts.

But that's not what I think about when I remember Ammie. I think about her elegance, her warmth, the fact that she read probably 90 percent of the fiction section at the Independence library. I think of her every time I have a glass of white wine. I think of her every time I choose my thumb over a paper towel to wipe away a splash of coffee. I think of her when I drape, rather than wear, coats over my shoulders—a thing she did often, a thing I equate with Old Hollywood, and with her.

20.
2001

I had just gone to the bathroom when the first person at school found out about the planes crashing into the Twin Towers. It was during class time, so the halls were near empty as I headed back to AP English. I saw Julie rushing to her locker when she spotted me. "Did you hear? They bombed the Twin Towers in New York City!" she said, almost accurately.

"What?" I asked, quickening my pace back to Mrs. Ruthers's classroom.

"I think all the teachers have it on TV," she said, rushing toward the other end of the hallway.

When I walked in the room, Mrs. Ruthers and my classmates were all staring at the screen mounted on the wall. I took my seat and joined the chorus of "Oh my God," murmurs, our hands over our mouths in shock.

Within about fifteen minutes, the teachers were ordered by the principal to turn the televisions off. Parents were calling the school in panic, many of them demanding their children not be exposed to any of the footage. Mom felt strongly the opposite. When I get home that day she gives me a long, hard hug and then rants about the school not letting us have access to information. We turn on the TV and watch the coverage from our living room.

George Bush's statement from an air force base in Louisiana is played over and over: "Freedom itself was attacked this morning by a faceless coward, and freedom will be defended . . . the United States will hunt down and punish those responsible for these cowardly acts."

That week is a blur.

We find out Mom's second cousin's husband was killed on one of the planes. I feel sick to my stomach with grief. I am curled on the couch—we are back in the Brooklyn Heights bungalow, which we will have for one more year before officially losing it to the bank—and Mom strokes my hair. We are watching some kind of celebrity fundraiser for New York.

"It's awful so many people died here, but I don't like what's happening with all this patriotic talk," I am sixteen and trying to make sense of my thoughts. "It sounds like we're going to war and that will just kill so many more innocent people."

Mom nods in agreement. "He's a hawk," she says. "The administration doesn't care because their children won't be the ones fighting and dying."

I begin to read the *Plain Dealer*—the same paper Mom is still delivering every morning at 3:30 a.m.—every day, and find myself in fervent accord with the editorials that criticize the call for war, the blind patriotism, the attempt to use the attacks as an excuse to hunt for more oil and "democratize" the Middle East through force.

Most of the kids at school either don't have much of an opinion or they are war-hungry too. I am surrounded by "proud Americans." I feel rebellious in my developing perspective. It is a little scary and certainly isolating, but it feels worth the risk. My bleeding-heart liberal French teacher, Madame Zelesky, becomes my closest ally. Mr. and Mrs. Ruthers, the history and English teachers, are also in my corner when I stop standing up for the pledge of allegiance, and when, a year into the war, I, without permission, hang up a posterboard in the hall that I write on with a Sharpie: "There is no flag large enough to cover the shame of killing innocent people.—Howard Zinn."

Something is happening and, looking back, it turns my stomach that my politicization had to coincide with such horror. But I suppose that is the case for most of us.

21.
"... a city to cover with lines ..."

"Break up the printing presses and you break up rebellion."
—Dudley Nichols

My great grandfather worked at a print shop in Old Brooklyn, right outside of Cleveland. I don't know much about him or about the shop but I do sometimes imagine the way the paper might have sounded in press on a machine built in the thirties. I never met my great grandfather, but when I imagine his hands gripping a big vat of ink, I picture a darker and more calloused version of his son's hands, my Gramps's hands.

After the cafeteria job, Mom worked at the print shop at a light factory for ten years, her best job to date, before she lost it during the financial crisis. Her job involved lifting, loading, carrying, copying paper, troubleshooting machines. The air in the print shop was always freezing, the noise was always loud, and eventually, it would leave her half-deaf. She also kept her newspaper delivery job for nearly a decade. She would arrive at the depot, compile the papers that had been printed moments prior, bag them, fill up her beat-up used Mazda, and go door-to-door, tossing newspapers into yards, or in allotted boxes, and, for the elderly subscribers, walking them to their door, sometimes bringing them groceries or shoveling their walkway when it was snowy. Her hands, I imagine, were always cold.

A boyfriend of mine in Chicago worked at a print shop where he would always wear an old-timey hat and talk like he was a turn-of-the-century prole. He was a Wobbly and taught me all about anarchist printers and communist newspapers, especially the Italian ones. His Chicago-Italian-1930s voice over-pronouncing *Sah-KO* and *Van-ZEH-tt-ee*, and the *Can-ZAH-ni Print-uh* (Sacco and Vanzetti, the Canzani Printer). He came to my bedroom, in the apartment I shared with a roommate, with ink-stained fingers, smelling of warm paper. His hair was silky, his eyes were blue, and the way he talked about the press was simply romantic.

I think about these histories when I used a Xerox copier to make my first feminist zines, when I teach about the importance of the printing press in the media studies classes I teach to college students, when I conjure the spirits of radical elders (like Ohio-born Dudley Nichols, who cofounded the Screen Writers Guild, like Albert and Lucy Parsons who operated an anarchist print shop in Chicago, like Cleveland provocateur d. a. levy and his mimeograph and "a city to cover with lines," and on and on . . .) who righteously exploited the press for liberatory propaganda. The mass duplicates, the ink creating images out of ideas, over and over in the machine and on my fingernails. It is real magic.

"The church and those in power made expert use of the printing press, weaponizing it to disseminate propaganda that declared magic and witchcraft inherently evil," writes feminist artist Jessica Caponigro. Depictions of naked women— haggard shrews and lusty temptresses—were warnings of Satan in human form. Later though, Caponigro notes, when the press was made more accessible to women, "depictions of witches became more complex and often reflective of real life." When the press became widely available, it became another tool of witchcraft—to manifest into being words and images that were once deemed impossible.

I think about the way the press and these hands of my family—blood and spirit—are imprinted in my DNA and in these pages. The dexterity of clicking on a laptop, that was a typewriter, that was a pen. The heat of brain and machine to create the duplicates of these words, these sentences, these paragraphs, these pages. I am full of this process even before it's happened, I think, because of my ghosts.

These legacies are such welcome hauntings.

PART 3

ALL OTHER WORK IS MERELY PREPARATION: LAKEWOOD AND COVENTRY ROAD

"It leads to each other. We become ourselves."

—Patti Smith

22.
Artificial Light

A few days after 9/11, I visit Kat's sister, Abby, at Starbucks. I walk in and she is talking to her coworker, Ben, who I think is cute. He has the same hair as the men in bands I am beginning to like, side-parted and in his eyes. He has tattoos and black spacers in his ears. He's older—twenty, I find out from Abby—and looks like an actual man. He's got stubble and he's tall.

"Raechel agrees with you," Abby says to Ben when she sees me walk in, then to me: "Raechel, Ben is also talking about how we're only going to war for oil. You two sound just like each other."

I am flush with excitement and embarrassment. I am not sure if I will be able to expand on my position exactly, but I am so excited we have the same one.

"You wanna take my smoke break with me?" he asks catching my eyes.

I shoot a quick glance to Abby, silently conveying, *Holy shit holy shit holy shit.*

"Yeah sure," I respond too casually.

Ben and I walk out to the sidewalk at Ridge Park Square, where Starbucks rests in a suburban strip mall. We are wedged between a Baskin Robins and a Verizon store, but with Ben next to me, the setting becomes infinitely cooler.

"So, fuck George Bush," he says lighting up and laughing.

"Seriously, fuck George Bush," I respond.

Ben launches into a diatribe about capitalism and war and white supremacy that I hear most of, but he is also muted and the ugly neon strip mall light transforms and surrounds him with what looks like an angel aura, and I am, in that instant, falling in love.

". . . and like, that's what the Food Not Bombs kids have been saying since the early nineties, you know?" His voice is coming back into focus.

"Food Not Bombs!" I am thrilled I recognize a reference he's making. "I just read about Food Not Bombs in *The Atlantic*!"

Being required to read *The Atlantic* by your AP English teacher is about the least-punk way to find out about Food Not Bombs, the anarchist group that feeds unhoused and hungry people with reclaimed food, but there we were.

Ben makes an understandable face. "Oh. OK . . ."

"Anyway, keep talking, did you say we have Food Not Bombs in Cleveland?!" I ask.

"Oh yeah, this older, like, ex-punk, Dirg, has everyone come to his shitty apartment to cook. Then they go to Public Square. Every Sunday." He takes another drag. I am so in awe of his insider knowledge.

"That's awesome," I say, body humming.

"So Abby said you guys went to Jimmy Eat World?" Ben asks about a band I love, who I am suddenly concerned that maybe I should not love.

"Yeah . . ." I say tentatively, trying to read Ben's face.

"They're okay, but kinda poppy now. There's this band Brandtson that is like them but, like, actually good," Ben explains and I nod, taking note. "They're playing a show at Speak in Tongues," he tells me and I am dying inside in anticipation of what might come next.

"Would you want to go?"

I end up not being able to go the show at Speak in Tongues, which is unfortunate because the Cleveland DIY space would close shortly after, but Ben asks me on an actual date a week later. We go see *Waking Life* at the Cedar Lee, the other theater that shows independent films and is around the corner from the Centrum, and then go to Tommy's on Coventry for veggie food (Ben is vegan; I still eat chicken and fish, but he'll persuade me with his homemade vegan mac and many trips to Soul Veg, and a year later I'll be totally vegan).

I feel confident on the East Side of Cleveland. It's alternative culture that I know well, which is dramatically different from the West Side alternative culture that is primarily white punks and/or goths who all seem to know everything about everything. East Side weirdos are broader, more diverse in age, race, class, interests. It's less constrictive, and feels truer to what I still have faith that punk and alternative offer us on the fringes of society: ultimately, belonging.

Ben orders a tempeh reuben. *"Temp-aye,"* I repeat silently the phonetic pronunciation of the vegan protein, in earnest study.

"So that movie was good, but, like, I am already annoyed at the people who see that and then think that they are suddenly philosophy PhDs," he says, taking a bite of his sandwich. "Like, I'm *in* a college philosophy class and it's not that movie."

I feel immensely mature. I have a boyfriend who is in college and we just had a date to see an independent film at the Cedar Lee and now we are eating at Tommy's and truly all my dreams have come true. After dinner we go to Mac's Backs Books, which is connected to Tommy's, and which envelops you with the smell of used paperbacks, challenges you to dig through the stacks to find what is waiting for you. Ben finds it. He calls me over, "Do you know Rilke?" he asks, holding the poet's book in his hands, "Rainer Maria Rilke, sound familiar?" I make the connection, "Like Rainer Maria, the band?" I say of a band we both like. "Yeah that's where they get their name." He flips through the book. "Listen to this," he says.

"It is also good to love," Ben reads, "because love is difficult. For one human being to love another human being:

that is perhaps the most difficult task that has been entrusted to us, the ultimate task, the final test and proof, the work for which all other work is merely preparation."

He glances up at me to see what I think. In response, I throw my arms around his neck and kiss him as hard as I can and I hope he can tell my tongue is saying *thank you*.

We go to Ben's parents' attic that night and he asks what record I'd like to listen to. "Wait—actually, I want to make sure you know about Le Tigre," he says. "I didn't end up putting enough women on the mixtape I'm making you, but I should have, and you need to know this band."

He likes teaching me and he's trying to be a responsible feminist ally. He plays their self-titled album, starting with "Eau d'Bedroom Dancing," which he tells me is his favorite song on the record. We make out heavily.

"I like this," I tell him sincerely between kisses, "the song I mean." I breathe while he moves to my neck. "It's so good."

"I thought you'd like it," he smiles, and kisses my mouth again.

After an hour of kissing and groping and rubbing and finally a blow job, we are lying naked in each other's arms staring at the ceiling.

The record is over. "What next?" Ben asks.

"You tell me!" I say, eager for more education. "I like these lady singers. You know, I've always thought the most romantic music is the music you hear in lesbian movies."

He laughed out loud.

"I'm serious! You know, like it's always this dreamy lady music," I continue, "like in *But I'm a Cheerleader*, that song when they first have sex is just the prettiest song in the whole world."

I had a now-unsurprising tendency to see all the gay movies. In the late nineties and early 2000s, LGBT-themed movies were primarily relegated to independent films, so I was especially excited to indulge not only what would later become my own sexuality, but also my love of low-budget cinema. I was most drawn to the lesbian stories, but Mom ate up a good movie about gay men falling in love and taking care of one another in their outcast communities, and we saw them all. *Broken Hearts Club*, *Jeffrey*, *Kissing Jessica Stein*, *But I'm a Cheerleader*. Unlike me, Mom wouldn't go on to realize she was queer, but it's no surprise she identified with these resilient, broken underdogs.

"'Glass Vase Cello Case,' I know exactly what you're talking about," Ben names the song and hops off the futon to his record collection.

The Venn diagram of indie/punk men and lesbian culture is a real one, and the center usually involves Le Tigre, Sleater-Kinney, and Gossip. For Ben, it also included Tattle Tale, the band featured in the aforementioned scene.

He's shuffling through his EPs. "Do you think you might like women too?" he asks nonchalantly.

I like the easiness of his inquiry. It motivates me to answer honestly. "You know, I think I'll want to make out with girls when I get to college."

"Just make out? Like when you're drunk? You know lesbians hate that!" he says. He knows a few. They've taught him.

"I don't know! I don't know yet, but I'm open," I say.

And I didn't know yet, that I'd meet Cam, and then, shortly after, Alice. That I'd go from 'maybe I'd make out' to falling desperately in love. I had no idea that I would discover new sexuality in Cam, broad-shouldered but hesitant, light brown skin and black coffee eyes, with the patch of a punk band I liked on her messenger bag. And that when we'd talk at the anti-war meetings, she'd be nervous and bumbly in a way that made me know she thought I was cute. How she had a haircut like a boy and dressed like a boy but had the softness of a woman and how that genderqueerness fucked me up. And how I'd tell my freshman year roommates that I had a crush and would they please come see her perform at the college talent show? And that when she strummed the Postal Service on her guitar, I melted, and thought, *Fuck, I am actually for-real not-straight.* How I'd flirt with her, how I'd invite her back to my college dorm and wrap my legs around her from a countertop, drinking vodka from a can of Diet Coke and telling her I wanted to attend the LGBTQIA campus group meetings, *you know, as an ally.* And she finally had some confidence after her Coronas with lime, and so her response was, "You're not an A . . . You're a B," and I shook my head and laughed and said *nooo* and then kissed her right on the mouth. And I didn't know that after I left that spring to live back in Cleveland for the summer that I would meet Alice, a quintessential riot grrrl with bangs and dinosaur tattoos and a love of the cutest girl music you'd ever hear (Tiger Trap, Go Sailor, the Softies, and others, all of which made it onto mixtapes she'd craft for me). She was also a tattoo artist, and she made me bleed so many times over, wiping wiping wiping away the blood from my skin as the needle gun drew lines of doves and roses and hearts and the outline of Ohio, before, during, and after our love affair. And when I got drunk on the Fourth of July in a Lakewood apartment, she made me cum quietly on a couch with her fingers and I knew I was in love and I knew I couldn't stay her girlfriend, not with her in Cleveland and me in Chicago, and not with me still being unsure if I could ever fuck her back . . . but I loved her all the same.

But I didn't know any of that when Ben asked me that question, and so I answered as best I could and then returned to him and his soft hair and the freckles that you could only see up close and his full lips and all his complicated maleness. And in that moment, I thought he was the most beautiful man I'd ever seen.

Ben finds the record: "Here it is." The opening chords begin. The song is literally perfect. He comes back over to the futon and kisses my face. "I think I'm supposed to say something about how I'd like to watch if you ever decide to be with girls."

We laugh. We kiss more. I am so in love.

23.
Closed Hands on Open Arms Hold Nothing

Things change very quickly. When we go from just dating to trying to actually integrate each other into our respective lives, it's a disaster. I invite him to my choir concert. He's awkward at the high school. He doesn't belong there, we both know it, and I'm suddenly embarrassed I invited him at all. And when I try to be part of his world, on the West Side, I become insecure, and he becomes mean.

The bridge I take to Lakewood is lit up in blue light, or at least it is in my memory. My palms sweat against the steering wheel when I approach it. West 117th is the exit I take to get to Ben's house, to get to Chris's Warped Records, to get to the punk house that people refer to as Fort Totally Awesome, to My Friends diner. I am still struggling to believe I have access to any of this. It wasn't so long ago that when Ben said "My Friends," I thought he meant his friends, like Molly's house or Davita's house. "We met at my friends," but he meant, "We met at My Friends." All the punk kids knew about it. It was the mom-and-pop Denny's, a way to have diner time without supporting a corporation.

People still smoked inside back then. So when I would exit on 117th and drive toward the train tracks and turn into the My Friends parking lot, I would prepare myself for the low air quality. I didn't smoke, but Ben did. I hated the smell of cigarettes, but I did like that his kisses tasted ashy.

I flip down my car shade and open the mirror to assess my eyeliner, my lip gloss. I stare up, the way I will stare at Ben in hopes that he'll be seduced by my mouth enough to forget that I'm not nearly as cool as him. I take a breath and head into the diner. I find him and he doesn't smile or really even acknowledge me, but he does see me.

"Hey," I sit down.

He flicks his cigarette.

"Hey. How are you?" he tries to be kind.

"I'm good, I mean school sucked today but," I already make a mistake with this. Ben is twenty and going to Cleveland State and I am in high school. He doesn't care about school and I don't need to remind him that I'm only sixteen and a half. "Well, never mind. How was work?"

"Well, my labor is exploited by a corporation and, like, is probably helping fuel the war machine, so pretty shitty," he spits out and laughs, almost in self-congratulation. He had a habit of doing this. Saying something really political, really fast, and then waiting for me to be impressed. I always was.

He takes a hit on his cigarette.

"Yeah. Capitalism is terrible," I attempt.

He's silent.

"So . . . I was listening to the mixtape you made me on the way here. I love it."

"Yeah, you told me that already."

"That Orchid song is like sooo . . . so fucking good." I keep trying. I won't give up.

"Yeah, I saw them in a basement in Kent like three years ago." He smashes his cigarette in the ashtray.

"Wow, that's awesome," I gush.

"Yeah, like, these Kent punks we met were weird, though. They like, they hate the internet, you know? Like they are total Luddites," he says in a way that is typical of this kind of exchange. He is eager to demonstrate how much he knows, how punk he is, and I am eager to affirm this.

I don't know what 'Luddite' means.

"Yeah man, that's weird," I say and force a laugh.

"I just think, like, technology is important for the revolution, you know?" he says quickly.

I'm smart enough to piece it together and say sincerely, "Oh, yeah, totally, I actually totally agree with that."

"Anyway, do you want coffee?" he asks.

I have told him at least a dozen times that I don't drink coffee and he knows that because I visit him at Starbucks where I order basically milkshakes.

"N—No. I," I can't believe I'm saying this. "I don't drink coffee."

He shrugs. "Then do you want to just go to my house?" I nod.

We go up to the attic. He puts on a Saetia record. The past few weeks, he stops asking what I want to listen to and just puts on a rotation of Saetia, Pageninetynine, and City of Caterpillar. Screamy hardcore bands (as opposed to regular hardcore bands, which Ben has taught me are distinct) have become very hot to me. I develop a near-Pavlovian response to lo-fi, high-pitched shrieks. My teenage hormones are out of control to make out with my cool punk boyfriend, to feel his fingers inside of me, to get a hickey from him. He still won't fuck me because I'm a virgin (and because he's twenty and I'm sixteen), but sometimes, with my permission, he puts just the head of his penis inside me and it's the most pleasure I've ever felt.

We sit on his futon. On this particular night, he's not in the mood to make out. I try to be sexy. He seems annoyed. Eventually we turn on a movie: *Buffalo 66*. He is Vincent Gallo and I am Christina Ricci.

Ben invites me to see Brandtson and Small Brown Bike at the Grog Shop. He's friends with Brandtson because Jill, who works at Chris's Warped Records, dates one of them. Ben is very proud of this connection. They are a local band that made it on to a prominent indie label and toured with some pretty big names, or at least big names in the world of music I now know about through Ben.

Ben half-introduces me to people at the show. I am suddenly very self-conscious in the corduroy pants I'm wearing. I took a risk and wore the pants I thought I looked hotter in rather than the pants that were hipper. But everyone else seems to be wearing a uniform that I didn't know was required: tight jeans (blue or black), black hoodies, and jean jackets or leather jackets over the hoodies. Because it's so cold, some people have on actual winter coats, but most of them chose fashion over warmth and they commit to their light jackets through winter. I make a note to ask my grandmother for a jean jacket for my birthday. I resent, though, that to fit in here, I may have to give up some of what is finally making me feel sexy.

When the music starts, I don't have to be anxious. Suddenly we are a mass of fans, not individual people with insecurities trying to shout small talk. The whole room is singing and clapping along. Ben has explained to me the value of a good hand-clap-breakdown in a song. "Hear that guitar riff?" he paused and rewound the tape in the car, like a football coach watching plays of Friday's game. "That's exactly when everyone's hands shoot up and they clap to the same beat. Happens at every show in Cleveland, but not always other places. Cleveland is pro-hand-clap."

I take note, I giggle, I clap on cue the next time the guitar riff comes in, and Ben laughs with approval. Those are the moments I feel like I'm getting somewhere. Like actually it's OK that I don't know all the things because he gets so much pleasure in teaching me.

So when Brandtson plays, I know what to do. And I genuinely love the music. I've memorized the album Ben recommended I buy. I know when to raise my hands in the air and clap with the guitar. I am part of this group and it feels like belonging in my bones; like the embodiment of the truest definition of the concept. I fit in this group, here, with these people, where we are all moved by the same thing, in a space where we are all part of something bigger. It is a feeling I won't get again until I am part of a political organization where we march in the streets as comrades. "It was like a fever": Francesca Polletta says that of protests, but I feel it at shows too. A washing-over, a heat that we generate together, a ritual for agitated teens who know there's something more than what we've been told to settle for.

But then the show is over. The music stops. The lights go on, and suddenly everything is unnerving again. Molly approaches Ben, giving me a side-eye but not actually acknowledging me. "Are you going to come to Pat's?" she asks pressing her hand against his chest.

"Uh," he glances at me, "I don't know, I'll try."

"You fucking better!" Molly says. She's drunk. ("Everyone loves Molly when she's drunk," Ben's told me before.)

Ben grabs my arm and pulls me toward the door. "I wanna go to Pat's, but I guess I have to take you home."

"I'm sorry," I say, "I can't go. I'm sorry you have to drop me off. But maybe you can go after?"

I feel so small. And, at the same time, like an enormous burden.

Ben doesn't say anything, just opens the door to the January air.

We walk quickly and silently from the Grog Shop to where the car is parked on the other end of Coventry. We get in Ben's car and sit in more silence. It's freezing. His breath and my breath are blowing like smoke in between our mouths and the frosted windshield. I will him to turn the car on, partly because I want the heat, and partly because I know he is mulling over how I am not good enough for him and I want him to have the distraction of driving. But he sits with his hands in his peacoat pockets and stares out toward the side mirror. He is thinking that this will not work. How he cannot be chained down by someone in high school.

"I'm sorry," I say again, meekly.

Finally, he turns on the car. The Weakerthans' *Fallow* album is playing. It is a breakup song. "I trace your outline in spilled sugar, killing time and killing hope," John K. Samson murmurs.

He takes me home. We are quiet the whole way. When we're in front of my house, he says, "I don't think this is working."

"I know," I say, a ball in my throat forming as solid mass.

I get out of the car. I pass my mom in the kitchen on my way to my room and weep in her arms. She cries as soon as I sink into her: "Oh, peanut, I'm so sorry." I don't have to say any words, she knows exactly what has happened. I peel away from her and go to my room. I sob. The loss of my relationship with Ben also feels like the loss of any hope I have to become who I want to be. Without Ben I don't know how I'll go to shows without feeling terrified. Without Ben I don't know how I'll learn the right anti-capitalist perspective on the news. Without Ben I don't know how I'll find out about new punk and hardcore bands. This all feels impossibly devastating.

My heart was decidedly broken and with it was a deep fear that I'd never be included in those spaces—punk houses, show venues, My Friends diner—again. Cleveland was small enough that it truly felt like Ben's friends were *it*. If you weren't part of the cool clique of punks and hardcore kids in Lakewood, you should probably just give up altogether. *I guess I'll have to wait until college to find my people again*, I lamented that night in my journal.

———————

When I become a feminist and when I am feeling very gay, I decide it is sad that I ever let a boy take up so much space. That I felt so dependent on him for my identity. But then I feel similarly overwhelmed and shattered by women and those who don't fit in the binary, and then I even feel this way about friends and I realize that of course I was in pieces when he left and of course I felt more whole with him, and her, and all of you.

In grad school, I will read Judith Butler. "Let's face it," she writes like she's nudging me with her elbow, "we're undone by one another. And if we're not, we're missing something." There's nothing truer, I will think, and I will summarize her in papers, that we are all, like it or not, contingent. We are as undone by one another as we are made up of one another. Ben taught me an articulation of anti-capitalist politics and opened up a world of punk music that stirred the part of my gut that knew I had found what I needed. I wouldn't have had that without Ben. Two years later, when I would meet Cam, the first butch lesbian I'd know, I would be similarly privy to a world of queerness made more real because I discovered it between kisses and the feeling you get in your belly when you're falling for someone. I am not embarrassed that Ben taught me more about myself than I'd have known without him. The same way no one would think it was strange that I knew my queerness more concretely through falling in love with Cam, I came to know my politics and my relationship to music through falling in love with Ben. We are not independent creatures in a vacuum—this I have known since my days of sharing food stamps and not calling the cops on the neighbors. Instead, we are constantly bumping up against one another, picking things up that we wouldn't otherwise, realizing what we love and who we are through someone else's experience of them. And this, I think, is more than just tolerable—it's a beautiful reminder that we need each other.

"I can only recognize myself recognized by the other," Jean-Luc Nancy writes, "to the extent that this recognition of the other alters me: it is desire, it is what trembles in desire." My becoming during the winter of 2001-2002 was entirely rooted in trembling desire—a desire for Ben, sure, but also for music that made me feel part of something, and for a politics that helped explain so much of what I'd already known (that the State wasn't designed to protect the most vulnerable among us). My desire for the records and the analysis was not so distinct from the desire for a boyfriend. And that winter I got all of it, all the desire I needed to settle more solidly into my skin.

24.
Swear I Way More Than Half Believe It When I Say That Somewhere Love and Justice Shine

Jackie is a good friend and she takes me to the movies the weekend after Ben dumps me, which also happens to be the weekend before my birthday. We go to Cinemark and buy tickets to *Spider-Man*. I think about how Ben would not want to see *Spider-Man*, how he's probably with Jill at the Cedar Lee seeing *Amelie* again, which we were supposed to see together for a second time. ("Jill cut her bangs just like that," he told me while we watch.) I am mopey because of all of this, but the truth is, I do want to see *Spider-Man,* and the truth is, I like the seats at Cinemark better than the seats at Cedar Lee.

As we leave the theater, we hear really loud music coming from a live band in the lobby. It sounds like stuff I like, it's pop-punky; you can't really understand the words. Jackie and I give each other a glance and walk toward the lobby to investigate. And then I see him. The singer is someone I've seen before. I place him quickly as having worked at the Parma movie theater, the "cheapie theater" where Mom and I would go to watch second-run films for only $3.50 a ticket. I get a flash of remembering his face behind the counter when I bought tickets for *The Craft*, of thinking after the movie ended that I wanted to cast a love spell on the cashier. *Did it work?* I wonder for a moment, because now, look—here he is again.

I explain this quickly to Jackie. She seems delighted that my mind is off of Ben. "Give him your number!" she demands. I feel sheepish and shy and know I won't have it in me to do that. But I do talk to him after and I try to make it clear I think he's cute—which he is, so cute, with sea-green eyes and big tattooed arms and a sweet smile that emerges when we talk. He invites me to another show they are playing a month later. I show up. He asks me on a date and I agree. Joey is kind and cute and into pop-punk. At this point, I know there is better punk than New Found Glory, but I don't mind that it's his favorite band. He's also into acting and does theater at school, which I do too. We have a lot in common. His family is also lower-income and his mom is disabled, and we bond about life not being easy. I am excited about him and everything feels right on paper and so it makes sense to become his girlfriend quickly. I also decide that it makes sense for him to be the first person I have sex with. It's not his first time. We light a candle. He is considerate and goes slow. The Get Up Kids play in the background.

Joey and I never really fought. There was no drama. I worry that that is perhaps why I decided early on that it would never last. I had already learned that love equals turmoil and when turmoil is missing, I begin to creep my foot slowly out the door.

———————

I'm feeling better and more capable and like maybe I can be a punk without Ben after all. Joey helps, sure, but I also focus on deepening my politics and finding new music on my own. I decide with great resolve that I will begin going to Food Not Bombs. I know Ben doesn't go, but that people he knows do. It feels both terrifying and exciting to think that I may run into people there who I'd met at shows with him. I wonder if they will remember me, or if they do, if they will say as much.

I have a flyer with FNB info that I've been saving since finding it at a show I went to with Ben a few months ago. It says to email to get the address of the apartment where they cook at 11 a.m., or to show up in Public Square to serve at 1 p.m. I am going to go all in, I think, and email when I get to the computer lab at school.

"Hello, I am interested in joining Food Not Bombs. I am against the war and have a passion for helping the homeless," I write, naively. "Please send me the address for cooking this Sunday. Thank you! Raechel."

Looking back, I am shocked they didn't think I was a cop.

Two days later I get an address. It's going to happen. I'm increasingly nervous and realize it will be impossible for me to go alone, so I ask Kendra, a friend of mine who is also anti-war and who is usually up for trying new things. I pitch her hard and even suggest we can use this toward our required community service hours for our honors program. She agrees.

We arrive at a small apartment in Slavic Village about ten minutes too early. I tell Kendra we should wait so we aren't the first ones there. We sit in the car and listen to a mixtape. Finally, we walk in, go up to the second floor, and knock. My heart is beating out of my chest. I don't actually belong here, I think, looking down at the jeans and Chuck Taylors that I hope will help me pass as legit. We open the door directly into the kitchen, which only has two people inside. I'm incredibly uncomfortable.

"Hi, we're here for Food Not Bombs," Kendra announces without concern. She's far less worried about how she's perceived. She doesn't have the weight of Ben's judgment on her shoulders.

"Oh," says the large white man at the table, probably in his mid-thirties, with a disheveled brown beard, giving us a bit of an annoyed look. "Did you email?"

"I did," I speak up, kind of raising my hand. "I'm Raechel."
"Oh," the man says.

Silence.

Thank god for John, the other man in the kitchen, who

extends his hand out and says, "Hh-hi-hhh-ii, Hi, I'm John, John." John has some kind of speech affect that makes him stutter a little at the beginning of a sentence and then repeat the last bit of it a second or third time at the end. He's pale, skinny, has an endearing floppy bowl cut, and wire-rim glasses. I like him and appreciate his welcoming nature. I shake his hand.

"Th-that-that that's Dirg. Dirg," he says, pointing to Dirg at the table, who doesn't react.

"They're just getting the food, so it should be back here to start cooking soon," Dirg says without making eye contact, trying to figure out what to do with us in the meantime. "Are you guys in high school?" he asks.

We nod. He softens a little. He clearly doesn't want to be a babysitter, but I get the sense that he knows it's his duty as an activist to help nurture the youth of the movement, as it were. "OK, well, we have some carrots from last week that are still pretty good so you can start chopping those if you want."

We are stationed in front of cutting boards on the kitchen table with knives and limp carrots, and although I am glad to have a task, I am suddenly terrified that I will chop incorrectly. I am in a cold sweat and tentatively place the knife near the carrot.

John steps in again. "H-h-here, here," he demos for me, "they don't have to be perfect, j-j-just any bite size pieces are good, are good."

"Thank you," I say sincerely, and begin chopping.

Soon more food arrives, carried up by two older teens. One looks pretty normal, and also friendly, I find out his name is Phil; the other is a classic-looking punk with a mohawk and studs on a patches-adorned leather jacket. He goes by the name Rabbit. A few more people show up, shuffling in and out, and although I don't quite feel like an insider, I feel calmer than when we first arrived.

A cat shows up in the kitchen and sits in the middle of the

floor, staring at all of us. I see it and rush over right away. "Oh hi, kitty!" I scratch her chin. "What's your name?"

"That's Emma," Dirg tells me, putting a pot of water on the stove.

"Hi, Emma!" I say back to the cat, then to Dirg. "Why 'Emma'?"

Half the kitchen stops and looks at me. This is a major rookie mistake. If you are in a leftist house with a cat and her name is Emma, you should know that she is named after Emma Goldman. But I didn't know who Emma Goldman was at this point, and this exposed me as a phony more than my clothes or my age or my awkwardness.

"Goldman . . . Emma Goldman?" Dirg finally says, incredulous.

My face is hot as I realize the room thinks I should know this.

"Oh, I . . . " I fade off, mortified.

Dirg had two options that morning. To write me off or to teach me. I am, to this day, so grateful he chose the latter.

He sighs heavily. "Come with me."

I follow him to the living room, where we stop in front of his huge bookshelf. He scans the shelves and stops on *A People's History of the United States* by Howard Zinn. "Here," he hands me the book. "If you promise to read this, and promise to bring this back next week, you can borrow this."

I know this is a big deal. Not only is he letting me borrow a book, but I get the sense that this book is full of the same things I learned through Ben, and now I get to learn it on my own. Plus, it's an invitation to come back.

"Thank you." I am near tears. "I promise I'll read it and bring it back next week."

After meal prep, everyone heads to Public Square. Kendra and I drive separately, with one of the Crock-Pots full of rice and beans in her back seat. We meet everyone in the center of downtown Cleveland that is surrounded by Tower City Shopping Center, the Ritz-Carlton hotel, and various pockets of poverty. In 2002, downtown Cleveland is near-vacant on evenings and weekends. The only people around are the shoppers, the hotel patrons, and hundreds of poor and homeless folks who spend their time trying to stay warm and pass the time. It's an ideal spot to set up shop with our warm food, but city officials disagree. Cleveland, like every other major city in the US, had been implementing "broken windows" policies that criminalize homelessness (and any evidence of it). Food Not Bombs managed to stay firmly planted in the square for decades. Today, I hear, they've been officially displaced. Food Not Bombs in Cleveland still thrives—two chapters even, one on the East Side and one on the West—but no longer in the plain sight of the downtown center.

But back in 2002, we met by the Sailors and Soldiers Monument that looms high in the center of the square. The punks of FNB perched on the stairs, mixed with the homeless and hungry folks. Regardless of their lot, most everyone was dirty; the FNB punks especially had a distinct odor that would overtake any basement or living room show. It was mostly body odor (deodorant was for capitalists, many would say) and garlic (the more, the better, was the general ethos). In my early days wading into FNB and punk culture, I did a lot of breathing through my mouth, but at a certain point, the smell became familiar in a way that made it neutral, and even pleasant sometimes. (Almost a decade later, during grad school in Minneapolis, I'd host two young punks who were in town for a conference and would whisper to my (very clean, ex-punk) partner, "It smells like Food Not Bombs in here." He knew exactly what I meant.)

The point—and what the punks aimed for—was to blur the lines. Unlike a soup kitchen with clean and tidy churchgoers who "serve the poor," FNB was about solidarity.

The bottom-line for FNB was not charity, but rather creating a world that didn't need the hierarchical divide between "haves" and "have-nots" to begin with. Taking food that would have been tossed out and using it to feed hungry people (the punks among them), preparing food in a punk house, and sharing it in "the commons" was all an explicit fuck you to capitalism. We didn't pay for the food, we didn't pay to rent a "proper" kitchen, and we didn't keep the eating behind closed doors.

Sure, some of these dirty punks were from the suburbs with rich parents, but not all of us. There are legitimate critiques about the whiteness and class privilege of a lot of radical punk spaces, but having been in it, I know it's not so monolithic. The radical left groups I would begin to immerse myself in in Cleveland, and go on to establish myself in in Chicago, were pockets of refuge for the real fringes of society. Homeless people (some who were young punks, many who weren't), people with mental illness who were ostracized elsewhere, queers, people who knew first-hand that hard work doesn't mean you'll be rewarded with a living wage—all of us were drawn to these meetings, the events, the gatherings with free coffee and people who didn't wear the right clothes. Cleveland FNB in particular was intergenerational and relatively diverse racially and socioeconomically. This isn't necessarily the norm for lefty punk spaces, but I was lucky enough to find my roots in one for which it was.

Admittedly, I didn't end up going to FNB for very long, but the Sundays I was there were actually life-changing. When I went to Chicago a year later, I was able to say I'd been involved in the group, which gave me an in with a local activist who would become a dear friend and mentor. The conversations, the Howard Zinn book, the quick awareness that we didn't like Democrats almost as much as we didn't like Republicans—all of it was the basis of what would go on to be the whole of me. Today, radical politics are as important to my identity as being queer, as being femme. It's as important as breathing.

My politics give me the only peace I can find when watching my hard-working mother dip further below the poverty line, when I grieve my queer Latinx best friend who died in a jail cell after being arrested for weed possession, when I worry with my transgender partner about whether or not a doctor will treat him properly. It is deeply personal. And if I didn't have the ideas and hopes and blueprints for alternatives that radical-left political communities compose together, I wouldn't have anything. "Hope is a discipline," says activist organizer Mariame Kaba. And for me, optimism only feels accessible when I'm engaged in praxis, making action of our theories, like publicly filling our bellies with the egregious excesses of capitalism's leftovers.

Those Sundays serving rice and week-old veggies and stale bagels in Public Square were one of the best things Cleveland ever gave me.

PART 4

CAN YOU STILL FEEL THE BUTTERFLIES?

"And that's how I choose to remember it."

—Rilo Kiley

25.
If Not Now, When?

Joey has a show at The Pit on Lorraine with How About No, a band he plays with regularly, and also a band called Driveway which neither of us had heard of. When you date a person in a band, it means you do a lot of standing around. There are a couple of women who either date, or are friends with, some of the other members of The Comix and How About No who are older and try to include me, which I'm grateful for. Parma punks are different from Lakewood punks. They are more inviting, less judgmental; I think some of it is about class, or perceptions of class anyway. There are low-income families in Lakewood, but they don't get written off as "trash" like folks in Parma do. Literally, people use the term "Parma Trash" to describe the city's mall-goers and restaurant workers and apartment residents. Unsurprisingly, I feel very comfortable there.

So, we wait for the bands to start playing. The boys load in equipment and talk to the sound check dude and occasionally stop over to check in on us. I like how much Joey likes me. He seems proud of me, and I know this whole scene is terribly unfeminist—girls and women waiting around for boys and men and feeling glad to be wanted—but it feels very validating at the time.

Once everything is set up, Joey comes to stand by me to watch Driveway, the opening band. I see one of the guitarists out of the corner of my eye and I feel my stomach drop. My eyes follow him as he gets ready on stage. I'm captivated. He doesn't look like the boys I've been into lately—he has blonde hair, not dyed black; he's wearing cargo shorts, not skinny jeans; he looks a little more normal. But when we lock eyes, it is the closest thing I've ever felt to love at first sight.

Their band plays and the music is good. The guitarist, whose name I will learn is Jack, is very good at playing guitar, but also seems shy on stage in a way that I find deeply endearing. I turn to Joey and announce, "I like this band a lot." He seems a little slighted. "Yeah, they're OK."

Once Driveway's set is over, I spend the whole night trying to spot my new crush. I try to be present when Joey is on stage, but I have a sinking feeling that I will have to break up with him soon, and I feel strangely certain that I'm going to be with this guitarist from Driveway.

Once the show is over, all the bands start loading their equipment into their various cars. At one point I am outside on the sidewalk in front of The Pit, covered in the orange-yellow light of the streetlamps, and Jack comes down the stairs with an amp. He stops when he sees me. It's just the two of us.

"Hey," we say almost at the same time.

"Hey," I say again. "I really loved your set."

"Thank you." He's pink-faced with my compliment.

"You play really well," I continue.

He's stammering, "I . . . I have to put this amp down."

"Oh!" I see his hands slipping on the big box, and grab the front of the amp. "Let me help you."

We walk the amp together to the car on the side alley. Once we're relieved of the amp, we are making conversation that I simply can't remember the contents of, but I do remember the feeling. The glow of the streetlamp, a dim dusk. I cannot understand why I am falling in love on that sidewalk but I am, with his goofy sideways smile and his big beautiful blue eyes.

Eventually Joey comes outside and I know I have to return to him. But before I go, Jack tells me his AOL name (@ CrashBmXpX) and I tell him mine (@everlove124). We will go home that night and find each other immediately. We will spend time on AIM talking about movies and music, which at this point is enough ground to build a relationship on. We will make plans to hang out as friends. He will tell me he has a beautiful view of Cleveland from the roof of his house in Garfield Heights and would I like to come over and see it? He will tell me, actually, he lives in a funeral home, just so I'm aware when I pull in. I will think it is all perfect.

Garfield Heights is only about ten minutes from Brooklyn Heights and I can either take the freeway or drive through Valley View to get there. I decide to take the longer way through the valley, to calm my nerves, to have more time with my mixtape. I know in my belly that I am driving to the next love of my life.

I arrive at Rajewski & Sons Funeral Home in the early evening. Jack tells me to park in the far side of the parking lot, in case there are any hearses that aren't yet in for the night. He assures me there are no visitation hours that day but there might be next time, and tells me that I'll have to walk past the casket room to get to their home, which is the second floor. I like that he already plans me being at his house again. "Don't worry," Jack says, "I'll come get you. Just text me when you're in the parking lot."

Jack always seems to be galloping. His movements are large. His voice is loud. He is shouting something to someone upstairs and he clunks quickly down the stairs and then the door opens and we see each other and our faces make hot, big, ugly, gaping grins. "Hi," I say and "Hi," he says, and we are stupid and standing and stuck. Finally, he grabs my hand and takes me upstairs, pointing out the visitation room, and then leading me up a narrow stairway that arrives at his dad's office. I meet Mr. Rajewski, one of the sons, who wears glasses that look like the seventies and who is very kind. Jack tells his dad that we're just going to hang out on the roof for a bit, and Mr. Rajewski warns us to be careful as we keep moving. His mom, Dee, is in the kitchen. She has lovely, sort of crimped, bright blonde hair. She has the same eyes as Jack and a sweet smile. We shake hands and she seems pleased to see her son with a girl.

We keep moving through the apartment, which is big, a little outdated, and a little messy, but still nicer than places I've lived. It's not intimidating, though, which I like. When we get to the living room, Jack introduces me to his little sister, Stephanie, who is sitting on the couch watching TV. I switch from parent-charm to little-kid-charm, and I'm not sure I've really mastered either, but everyone has seemed receptive so far.

"Steph, we might want the TV later," Jack says before taking my hand again and leading me to the window that will take us to the roof.

Finally, we get to the top of the building, which is flat and perfect for stargazing, or really small-city-light-gazing, and we get a dreamy view of downtown. Jack and I talk easily—about our families, more movies we love, more music we love, books we're reading. He makes me promise I will read *Perks of Being a Wallflower,* which I had heard Ben mention with disdain for being another thing that would make people think they understood subculture without really understanding it. Jack is not disdainful; he is earnest. So, so earnest. It's much more comfortable for me to be with someone who isn't afraid to love something without irony or critique.

We are also finding every excuse to touch each other. He set a good precedent with his decision to lead me around the apartment with his hand on mine, and our skin keeps asking for more of it. We are sitting side by side, looking past the residential clutter and occasional fast food or gas station sign toward the tip of the Terminal Tower that penetrates the Cleveland skyline. He tells me he wants to be a filmmaker. I tell him I want to change the world but that I'm not sure how quite yet. He tells me he has a cool aunt who is a vegetarian

Buddhist nun, but that he is very Catholic. I tell him I have a cool great-aunt who is a lesbian, and that I am still figuring things out when it comes to religion. He tells me more about his sisters (he has three, but the other two are away at college). I tell him more about my mom and what happened to my dad. He looks at me heavy when I explain this part. I am used to this response, the pity look, but with Jack it feels truly tender. I'm so sorry, he says. It's OK. I mean it's not, but thank you, I say, and use it as an opportunity to lean my shoulder against his. Our fingers graze. We are erupting inside. We are quiet but can hear our hearts beat against our chests, can hear our shaky breath.

"You know I have a boyfriend?" I say after a long pause.

He sighs and closes his beautiful eyelids. He moves just an inch away from me, just enough so our skin is now separate. The energy of our touching deflates like a dead tire.

"I do, I know," he says.

"I like you so much," I say.

He likes me so much too, he says.

I decide for certain that I will break up with Joey.

26.
Feminist / Dyke, Whore /
Pretty, Pretty / Alien

This is the summer I decide that I am mad at punk. I still love the music, but I'm angry at the culture for pushing me away from femininity. Do I even like Chuck Taylors? Are Chuck Taylors even comfortable? I am just barely at a place where I'm willing to show my legs in public, but now I feel beholden to jeans with studded belts. How can something make me feel so utterly like myself and also so far away from myself? How was I ever supposed to feel confident at a show if I was either wearing something that wasn't punk enough or something that was punk, but androgynous in a way that made my skin crawl? I want to be hot like Jill from the record store—tall, skinny, beautiful Jill—who was so naturally stunning that she could wear black T-shirts, jeans, and Converse and look amazing. I am short. My body is proportioned in the wrong ways. My face, I have decided, looks pretty good with makeup, but I am starting to get the sense that if I wanted to be a good feminist—which was feeling increasingly important to me, and seemed to also be to some punks—then I shouldn't be concerned with makeup?

The subculture sends me mixed messages—women in music videos of some of my favorite pop-punk bands look exactly like the most popular skinny blonde cheerleaders at school, except maybe they are wearing a midriff polo from PacSun instead of from Abercrombie. I will never look like a hot cheerleader, so that's not a feasible option. I continue to look to indie films for inspiration, but I still don't feel like I can pull off "sullen hot" the way Thora Birch does in *Ghost World* or the way Zooey Deschanel does in *The Good Girl*.

There is a type of hot that is hot because it is effortless, and I know I will never obtain it. I tried it in middle school with the Abercrombie shirt Nana bought me, with Sun-In to make my hair blonder, with my finger down my throat to make my stomach flatter. And when my bald spots didn't grow back in, Mom took me to a hair extension salon for kids with cancer and other hair-loss-resulting illness, and I picked bleached-blonde strips to be glued into my mousy brown hair. But these were pyrrhic victories. I felt just as insecure, just as itchy with the name-brand shirt, the blonde hair, the flat stomach. And they were also a lie: effortlessness took so much work.

Suddenly Ammie, my stunning, glamorous grandmother, comes to mind. There was nothing subtle about Ammie—her dresses were costumey, her makeup was pronounced. Her shoes—always her *metallic gold* shoes. But also, it seemed easy. It was effort she enjoyed, effort that was natural.

This was not so different from the girls at school who left in the afternoon to go to cosmetology classes at the vocational education center. They made an effort: layers of makeup, the daily use of straighteners and curling irons, the piercings and tattoos. They were decorated, adorned, and unapologetic about all of it. At school, the Coz (cosmetology) Girls were considered trash. Almost none of them lived in Strathmore, but collected on the edges of the development on the hill, in the same places I lived—the bungalows of Brooklyn Heights, the low parts of the Valley, and some by the sewage plant in Cuyahoga Heights. Without family money, college wasn't a given, and so voc-ed classes made sense. Plus, they loved hair and makeup.

I always had a feeling that if my dad hadn't been hit by the car—if we had stayed in the Valley, if I had spent more time with my dad's side of the family (especially with my cousin

Jennifer, who I admired so intensely as a kid and who would later go on to literally model on muscle cars in a bikini)—that I might have been a Coz Girl too. I never joined in on the jokes about their bleached-blonde highlights, their layers of makeup, their piercings and tattoos. In fact, I envied their boldness. They knew who they were, and they weren't sorry about it. Like the women at the racetrack, like the women who knew they were always already doomed to fail the tacit respectability test—so why not just lean into the immodesty, the excess?

With all of this swirling in my mind, I decide I will lean into my roots. To Ammie's theatrics, to the white trash that broke decorous femininity, to the deliciousness of non-alienated labor that is putting on your face, teasing your hair, finding the dress that makes you finally breathe easy.

27.

Spectacular Views

I end things with Joey in July, almost exactly three weeks after meeting Jack. It is sad, but I know I am in love with Jack in a way that makes it feel literally impossible to be with anyone but him.

The first night I am single, I return to the rooftop of the funeral home with Jack, but this time we kiss and kiss and kiss and kiss until our mouths are nearly numb. He is a sloppy kisser, but I love it, and him, and how his hair feels in my fingers. I am eager to do more right away, and my hand finds his cock above his shorts. He grabs my arm and pulls it away and I get the sense that this will move slowly. I don't try to touch him again that night, but I want to.

The rest of the summer is actual magic, by which I mean it is nearly unbelievable in how it unfolds like we are in an actual love song, surrounded always by breathtaking sunsets and skies full of stars. We spend nearly every day together. He visits me at my job at the Gap. He is so kind to my mom. We go to shows, mostly local ones, at least once a week. I meet and love all his friends, and he loves mine, especially Kat, which makes me very happy. We watch movies and make out and talk about how films and music and books make us feel less alone and how, when we like the same films and music and books, it makes us feel instantly connected to one another. We discuss this as though it is novel, we are so excited to have figured this out. We talk about the war and Food Not Bombs and I ask him to go with me sometime. He's no anti-war activist, but I can tell he's sympathetic, and a few months later he will play a Bright Eyes song on repeat and passionately sing along when Conor Oberst shouts, "Well, ABC, NBC, CBS: bullshit

/ They give us fact or fiction? I guess an even split / And each new act of war is tonight's entertainment/ We're still the pawns in their game / As they take eye for an eye until no one can see /We must stumble blindly forward, repeating history."

By August we have done everything but have penetrative sex. Jack's family is so Catholic. I attend church with them sometimes. He is just so deep in it. He thinks he may go to hell if we have sex. I try to be understanding—in fact, sometimes I wonder if it is true that we will. I am still toying with the idea that on the off chance there is a hell, maybe I should make decisions to avoid it. The problem is that when it comes to sex, it is too late for me, and so I have less to lose. I don't remember pressuring him exactly, but it's possible I did. But one day after we both cum from means other than his penis in my vagina, he announces that he thinks he may be ready to have sex with me because, he says, holding my head in his palms, "I'm in love with you."

My stomach drops and I kiss him so hard. "I'm in love with you too, Jack." I kiss his face, "I'm in love with you so much."

Jack plans a special night for our first time. He takes me to what feels like a fancy Italian restaurant, tucked in a strip mall near a grocery store in Parma. We both dress up. I put a fake flower in my hair, feeling dainty, and a studded bracelet around my wrist, finding a balance between my subcultural proclivities and my gendered ones. He whispers about how stressful it was to buy the condoms that day. I hold his hand across the table. We smile at each other a lot. He has this habit of looking away nervously and then knocking the wind out of me with a stare a moment later. He is this mix of confident and insecure that taps into my desire to both caretake and be taken care of.

We have sex in my room in the attic. It is very good. Like—surprises me how good it is. His cock fills me in a way that makes me close to cumming with barely any effort. We become pretty ravenous for one another. We have sex a lot, but sometimes we'll also talk about God and sometimes we even pray for forgiveness after. About a month into us having sex, his parents find a receipt for condoms. It's a devastating blow to them, and so also to our relationship. He calls me on the phone, sobbing. They don't want him to see me anymore. We are both crying. I say I'm sorry. He says he is too. Thankfully this passes within a couple weeks—he gets his sister involved to help talk to his parents. I talk to his parents. I don't remember if there were any promises that we would stop, but of course we didn't.

The air in the funeral home is heavy, and we both know it's from the dead. There are many days I come over and pass the visitation room when bodies are inside. Sometimes I wonder if my relationship with Jack is saturated with the lost love of those passed. That perhaps the romances that live in their unbeating hearts float up through the ceiling and into the Rajewskis' living room and when we kiss, we are breathing them in and out with us: past lives, but ones that aren't our own. Sometimes I wonder if that's why it felt so intense, so certain. Were we carrying the love stories of the dead? Maybe our love was this thick because it wasn't just ours.

By Christmas, I am back in his mom's good graces, and his dad no longer avoids eye contact. Jack gets a tattoo for his eighteenth birthday, which is early in December. It is a lyric from a Jimmy Eat World song, and for a moment he will connect it to our love: "Can you still feel the butterflies?" Yes, forever, we insist.

I am happy, I realize somewhere in the midst of this, because I am comfortable—deeply comfortable, with myself, and importantly, with myself in relationship to another person—perhaps for the first time in my life. My love for Jack is also love from the spirits in the funeral home, and divinely, love for myself, this person I have clawed my way into being. A young woman, it would seem, who has a bit of herself figured out.

In the midst of this, Mom and I officially lose the Brooklyn Heights house and she has to declare bankruptcy. We find an apartment in Parma, which I find to be a little depressing, but I'm trying to be a mature adult and at this point I want Mom to know I'm proud of her for always figuring out how to make it work, even if "making it work" is a shitty apartment. It's run-down and there are multiple big buildings in a giant parking lot. Abby guesses it's a hub for drug deals. The poverty manifests differently here than in Valley View. For one, the residents here are not mostly white people. Not unrelated, the cops are around more often. I'm not comfortable here, I admit to myself with a little guilt, and I play track one on the new Postal Service album over and over and over: "You seem so out of context / in this gaudy apartment complex." Me too, I think.

But Mom, as always, makes joy there. The two bedrooms are tiny, but at least there are two of them. We buy discounted patio furniture for our "dining room" (which is also the living room). The kitchen is basically a small hallway. But every week, Mom and I make a new vegetarian recipe she finds for us on VegWeb and prints out at work, and every week we watch *Dawson's Creek* (we love Jen, hate Joey) and the *Gilmore Girls* (we love Lorelei, are annoyed by Rory), and every Sunday, Abby comes over for a ritual viewing of *Sex & the City* (collectively, we like Samantha and Miranda best). It's one year of my life, I remind myself, and really it's not so bad.

Because we're in Parma, our address is an issue for the school again. We cross our fingers that I can finish my senior year without a problem, but I am called to the office one afternoon and they ask me questions and I am crying and I tell the truth, which is that we live in Parma, it's true, but my dad, he still lives with Frances in Valley View and no, we have no more legal binding really, but he's still my dad isn't he? (Isn't he?)

This is a small town. The principal likes me. We are white. No one gets sent to jail. I'm allowed to graduate.

That I would leave Cleveland to go to college felt inevitable. Not because I hated Cleveland, not because I hated my family, but because in the early years of my life, I had so many reasons to escape it. My survival-based daydreams of a life beyond Ohio became the blueprints of a future.

My friend Colleen, who is a year older than me, goes to Loyola in Chicago and tells me I'd love it there. Even after several years of thinking I was destined for New York City, Chicago sounds the most right, and Colleen being there makes it feel a lot less scary. After a visit to DePaul University, I know it's where I'm supposed to be. The price doesn't even make sense to me—it's an amount of money I can't wrap my head around, but I, like so many of us, assume it will be something I can easily pay back after getting the kind of good job one would get after getting a degree. Growing up surrounded by people who didn't go to college (and the few who did, with success stories to show for it), I really thought I was playing the game right. Go into debt now, but find yourself on the other end of your bootstraps after. Mom and I don't know how to do the FASFA, but we try. We get only a little scholarship money. Most of it is loans. Given how little she made, I think we must have messed up the paperwork. Mom can't afford to put the security deposit in for the dorm though. For a moment I wonder if this won't happen after all. But then one day in her kitchen, Ammie opens her purse and writes a check. Uncle Dana says he will help too. They are going to help make this work. At least enough to secure a dorm room, and another few thousand each toward the tuition. This is not a thing all poor people have. This is my privilege. And I still finished school with over $50,000 in debt. This was my choice, but if we're honest, I didn't fully grasp the weight of it. How could I?

Senior year, I feel secure in myself and am overwhelmed with appreciation for my friends, especially Kat. I love her quiet humor and her gorgeous smile. I love the way I hear her voice mix with mine in the car when we are singing along to Rilo Kiley. I love that she is introverted and particular in a way that makes me feel lucky for her energy and that she picks me over and over. (A decade later, she will still be my sister, my family, and she will have three beautiful babies and they will call me Aunty Raechel and I will feel so grateful to know someone who has known my whole life, who was able to see my mom when she was at her best, who understands what it means to have been on the poor end of the spectrum at our high school and to have turned out pretty fucking well anyway. She still has the most gorgeous smile. She is still particular and I still feel lucky she's picked me.)

28.
The Hum of the Electric Air

By early spring things are volatile with Jack. We are fighting a lot now. We fight about things that don't matter (I can't remember a single example of the content of our fights, but I remember how often they began to happen). Mostly, we are both stubborn and needy and emotional. One night, he leaves the apartment in Parma with a threat to walk home to Garfield, which wouldn't be impossible, but it'd be dangerous on mostly sidewalk-less roads. I chase him through the parking lot toward the street. It is dark and we are both crying. It's dramatic and scary and I am so angry and also, this chaos is familiar.

In one of the periods when Jack and I are on a break, I start hanging out with Ben again. I am infinitely more confident than the last time we had spent time together, and he notices. I'm still not as cool as him—the bands Jack and I listened to together are still poppy by comparison to Ben's tastes—but I am eighteen now and I have the allure of a woman in an on-again, off-again relationship.

Ben and I talk about being just friends. We think this is a great idea. He invites me over to his new apartment, which he shares with Ethan, and who looks like a punk version of Devon Sawa. The living room is lit by a table light with no lamp shade, which sits on the floor. The dark spring night pushes up against the window, but inside, the yellow glow turns our surroundings into something soft and hushed, something dream-like. I still almost never drink but at Ben and Ethan's house, the cheapest white wine seems irresistible and I get tipsy with them on their couch listening to The One AM Radio split with Tracy Shedd, who is an airy, lo-fi lady singer, just like I like.

"I like this chick's voice," Ethan says.

"You and Raechel and your lesbian movie soundtrack dreams!" Ben shakes his head and I laugh, proud of this inside joke that even Ethan doesn't know about.

There's the sound of footsteps coming up the stairs and Ethan announces that Eileen and Zack are coming over. I get instantly nervous because Eileen is the most gorgeous person I have ever seen and everything I want to emulate aesthetically and she scares the shit out of me. I admire her for choosing hotness. I mean, there is no mistaking that she's a punk, but also she's sexy. And she's not going to wear a hoodie when she could wear something cute and off-the-shoulder. I take so many mental notes. And I drink another glass of wine in a way that makes me suddenly understand why people drink and how it could become a problem.

Eileen and Zack walk in and Eileen shoots me a look, disappointed—or really more annoyed—that I'm there. I touch Ben's leg for some confidence. I'm here with him. Even though we're just friends, I know he wants to fuck me and I let that drive me through the night. Ben's knee rests into the cup of my palm and he inches a little closer. The desire feels powerful. Not his desire, but mine. The desire for his desire and that I obtained it. I'm leaning in to this kind of sexuality—and contingently, an amplification of my femininity—even more now.

Eileen, who is gorgeous with freckles and dyed black hair and swoopy bangs and a big banana tattoo, Zack, who is very skinny, Ethan, who looks like Devon Sawa, and Ben and I sit around in the living room, everyone except me and Ethan smoking. Ben is talking about voting with your dollar.

"That's the only thing that will make a difference," he says, his cigarette hand in the air in emphasis. "You have to show the corporations that you won't buy things if they are sweatshop-made or not fair-trade or whatever else."

I am, as usual, wildly impressed—though years later I'll decide this analysis is weak because there is no ethical consumption under capitalism. Everyone is getting drunker and more distracted during his rant, but I am focused on him. At one point Zack suggests we all drink in the bathtub. Ethan and Eileen agree this is a great idea.

"Let's go to my bedroom," Ben whispers in my ear.

Ben's room is right next to the bathroom, so we hear the tub fill and drunk voices and spilling beer. We are making out heavily on the bed. It's so different now. I am not a virgin, I am eighteen, I don't *need* Ben the way I did before. I rub his cock over his black jeans (I've never seen him in, or touched him in, anything other than black jeans).

"Hey is this OK?" he asks me.

"Is it OK with you?" I ask back.

"I thought we were gonna be friends?" he laughs.

"We are. Friends who have sex," I say back. I feel powerful as shit.

"OK," he kisses me, "I like that."

We have sex the way an eighteen and twenty-two year old would have sex. It's good, not great but I don't know the difference really. I do know that it doesn't feel as tender or special as when Jack is inside me. And I cum easier when I fuck Jack. Probably because we're always sober, probably because we're in love in a way that, looking back, reminds me to believe teenagers' feelings. I think about how I am in love with Jack in a way that will stay with me, and how I love Ben too in a way that will stay with me, but that it's very different. Ben I admire. Jack I want to take care of. I feel thrilled at eighteen to know such different ways of wanting.

"I have a new record for you to fall in love with," Ben announces after we've both cum. He stands up and goes to the record player, "Mirah."

Mirah's *You Think It's Like This but Really It's Like This* plays and Ben is entirely correct. It shakes my bones. It's perfect. I listen to it on repeat the end of my senior year and all of my first year in college. I will go on to see Mirah play a show in a big loft in Chicago and I will make friends with people—queer women in particular—in college because of our common love of her and I will reflect gratefully on the night of the bathtub party. (I will, eventually, reflect gratefully on how Ben was really a teacher for me in how to woo those queer women too.)

Ben invites me to a show at Fort Totally Awesome, the DIY house show space in Lakewood, a few weeks later. I don't know it then, but it will be a show that will give me major cred a decade later when the band becomes huge. At the time though, Against Me! was a punk band far enough under the radar that it still played in tiny venues. Ben put a song from their first full-length album, *Reinventing Axl Rose*, on the mixtape he made me. It was one of my favorite songs on the whole tape. So when he says this band from Florida was doing a tour and that Fort Totally Awesome's basement is on their schedule, I am very excited.

At the show, I am still insecure around all the people there who look cooler, more comfortable, more punk than me, and of course Eileen is there with her perfect bang swoop and freckles and banana tattoo. As usual though, when the music starts, everything is OK. We file into the basement, which is overflowing to the point that you can't actually get down the stairs at a certain point. Ben and I make it down for a second, but I can't see anything and I feel like I might get trampled, so after I hear the song he put on my mixtape ("We Laugh At Danger (And Break All the Rules)"), we head back upstairs and listen from the living room, which is also completely packed, and we stumble into a conversation about the war with some other people in the living room.

Suddenly someone runs upstairs in what should have been a panic but sounds more like an exclamation of accomplishment: "Everybody out! The floor beams are cracking!"

There isn't immediate movement at first, but some older and less-excited-sounding people emerge and confirm this is true and that we really need to get the fuck out of the house. Some people leave, Ben and I head to the porch. Lakewood is a city of porches. Everyone I know in the affordable part seems to have some kind of stoop, and in the early summer like we're in now, the laughter and smoke and sipping sounds of people on their respective front yard enclosures create a gooey static that wraps its arms around me. Here on the Fort Totally Awesome porch, Ben smokes and lots of people drink and most people talk, but I am quiet and observing and looking at the part of the Cleveland skyline you can see from Lakewood and it's almost like the lightning bugs that night are brighter than the streetlamps and I decide that this, this, this is the Hum of the Electric Air and I am overwhelmed with gratitude to hear it.

29.
Ooh Do I Love You

Jack and I are back together but still full of drama. We get in a fight before prom pictures and I cry so much I have to redo my eyeliner in the car. We decide that when we get to Chicago for school, we will not be officially together. We want time and space to do college right, not tied to a high school relationship. So we are together, kind of, creating conflict, I think, to make it easier to not be together in just a few months. But even when we fight, our love is still rooting us in deep care for one another.

One afternoon he is at the apartment and Mom isn't home. We are hanging out in the living room, wasting time before going to meet his sister and her boyfriend at the mall. There is a knock at the door and I answer it.

It's Ron.

"Sorry," he starts to walk away. "I thought your mom was home, sorry."

I'm frozen. He turns around again and walks back toward me. I nearly choke. But I am still frozen. Before he gets too close, I am able to shout, "NO."

He stops. "Sorry," he says again. He leaves.

Jack is behind me at this point, and sees Ron walk away.

"Is that . . . ?" he asks. I have told Jack, just briefly, about what happened. I have an easy narrative for it at this point. I talk about it with the same distance I do when explaining my dad's accident. *My father was hit by a car when I was four. My mom's boyfriend held me on a bed when I was twelve.* They are just sentences in my story, no more, no less.

I manage a nod, still standing at the door.

Jack's face is red. He is nearly shaking.

This jolts me out of my triggered freeze.

"Baby, what's wrong?" I hug him.

"I hate him," Jack says. Then suddenly, he is crying. Big tears falling out of his beautiful tender blue eyes, "I wish I could kill him, I hate what he did to you."

I remember this so vividly because it was the first time in my absolute entire life that a man made me feel like he wanted to protect me. Like I could rely on a man to keep me safe. Like a man cared enough to want me to be free from harm, rather than cause it.

My heart sinks. I cry with him, us holding each other. I couldn't believe what this felt like. I wanted to feel it forever.

I will do a lot of unpacking of that wanting. In therapy, in journals, with tarot decks. It became so clear to me in that moment how much I wanted to be protected. How blatantly I was falling, and would continue to fall into expected narratives of girls without fathers looking for their Daddy in every romantic relationship. It doesn't matter the gender, I seek it— being taken care of, a semblance of armor in whomever I find to love me. When I realize that this is something I want, but not something that I need, I will be OK with this desire and also the nature of it.

30.
I Get By with the People I Know

*"Men and women might mistake us [femmes] for 'just girls'
when they see our makeup and fashions, but we were/are actually
guerrilla warriors, fighting undercover in the war to save women
from the continuing campaign to make us irrelevant fluff."*
—Jewelle Gomez

The end of the school year and the summer that follows are slow motion, and every song is for me, and for everyone I love, and the nights all seem to last forever. I am more solidly myself than I ever have been, confident in this new future chapter of a life in Chicago. My body changes it seems, not physically, but in the way I carry myself. I see it when I look at pictures from senior year. How my shoulders were higher, how, with a grown-out pixie cut, I look so much like my grandmother.

I buy a rockabilly dress from Hot Topic for the spring choir concert. It is black with tiny red stars all over it and a halter neck. The corset-like bodice gives me cleavage I don't really have, and the A-line skirt puffs out with a little bit of tulle underneath. I learn about Suicide Girls, a soft-porn site featuring tattooed punk and goth women, and imagine what I might look like in the dress if I had tattoos and longer hair, which I promise myself I'll finally grow out. For graduation, I buy an all-white strapless pencil dress from Express. Ammie tells me I look like a vision when she sees me try it on, and I actually believe her. She beams at me and I beam back at her. (*I got it from you, Ammie*, I think to myself.) For both events, I wear my favorite high heels—black with a little bow at the peep-toe. I feel sexy. *Sexual*. No word for it yet, but later, yes: femme.

"Femme," I would learn later, was a term that emerged through the early gay bar culture in the 1940s and '50s. These bars in the cities were filled with queer people, but importantly, they were also working-class people. The only reason they were able to congregate at all was because they were working menial jobs—butch women often drawn to the kind of factory work where they could wear gender-neutral clothing, and femme women drawn to secretary jobs that didn't require higher education. Historian John D'Emilio explains that although queer behavior has essentially always existed, it required the material conditions of capitalism to enable, as a cohesive political category, queer *identity*. And, controversial as it may be on the Left, I'm firmly in the camp that believes identity matters. How identities are enabled or constrained is a reflection of the power imbalances of the State, not a frivolous distraction from them. With the butches and femmes of the early twentieth century, we witnessed the happy autonomy of their dialectic; forced to work to live, sure, but also free to congregate (and fuck each other and fuck with gender).

Femme, in particular, was a version of femininity that was socially acceptable insofar as it was legible, but it was formed by the working poor, and it wasn't for men. Rather than appeasing the male gaze, femmes got dressed for the pleasure of their butches and for the pleasure of their own damn reflection in the mirror. And it was, or became, a little exaggerated. More lipstick, higher heels, tighter sweaters. A femme instinct to up the sex appeal to better spite the male gaze. Ultimately, this kind of femininity—excessive and not for men—was punished. Sometimes overtly, when gay bars would be raided and queers of all genders would be beaten and thrown in the backs of police cars. And sometimes more subtly, as by the middle- and upper-class women who turned their noses up at the breast-hugging blouses, short skirts, big hair.

"The working-class woman personifies the 'slut' and so functions as ground to the middle-class figure of respectability," scholar Nadine Hubbs writes, "In fact, respectability exists only as a function of class distinction. It emerged historically as 'a property of middle-class individuals defined against the masses.'"

My femme ancestors were never afforded access to respectability, and they became the vanguard for us to be entirely OK with that.

Dolly Parton is not queer, but there are few above her on the list of agreed upon queer icons, particularly for drag queens and femmes. She told a story once about the "town tramp" in the small Tennessee town where she grew up poor: "I make jokes about it, but it's the truth that I kind of patterned my look after the town tramp. I didn't know what she was, just this woman who was blonde and piled her hair up, wore high heels and tight skirts, and, boy, she was the prettiest thing I'd ever seen. Momma used to say, 'Aw, she's just trash,' and I thought, That's what I want to be when I grow up. Trash."

Not all femmes identify as trash, and being trashy doesn't mean that you are necessarily femme, but their commonality is a salient one, which is that they are both in the practice of embodying the deviant. In *Not Quite White: White Trash and the Boundaries of Whiteness*, Matt Wray suggests that white trash positionality is a kind of in-between space in which the racist myth of white supremacy is made suspect through the disobedient poor whites who do not behave the way they ought to. Wray notes: "In conjoining such primal opposites into a single category, white trash names a kind of disturbing liminality: a monstrous, transgressive identity of mutually violating boundary terms, a dangerous threshold state of being neither one nor the other." Like the glowing lightning bug carcass, neither dead nor alive, persevering in a way that is as beautiful as it is grotesque.

And so, yes, I've come to use that word in an act of reclaiming. To celebrate the ways I and the women who raised me defied the logics of Whiteness, a construct we all ought to be working to dismantle. I'm not saying the women I was surrounded by had any sense of this, nor that they don't still benefit from white skin privilege, but their unfit bodies and sensibilities were something I would later learn were undesirable, and that eventually I'd want to be undesirable too if it meant I didn't abide an oppressive system. And I was swimming in admiration for these women who were white, but not the right kind. They were overabundant in everything but cash, and I felt absolutely cradled by it.

The femmes who had to work in turn-of-the-century cities to survive under capitalism weren't so different. The ones who, upon situating themselves in their skirts and blouses on a chair behind a desk in an office above a factory floor, would catch the eye of a butch worker. The ones who discovered the possibility of pleasure in female masculinity. They were the femmes who left work to meet up with the butches at the bar. To make out in a bathroom or on the dance floor. And then, later, to take off their heels to throw them at the cops who beat their lovers for wearing more than one piece of men's clothing. They were the Black, white, and Brown women who learned not only to endure capitalism, white supremacy, and heteronormativity, but to find joy in spite of it. They were the poor and scrappy women. Women without whom I would be genuinely less free.

All of them—the queer femmes I've known only when I'm kneeling in some version of prayer, the beautiful trash I grew up around, and also, Ammie—they are in and of me in ways that help me remember that we are so contingent. Their hyperfeminine excess, all costume glamour and trashy tattoos, is how I "do" my queer femme today. Gender is a performance, and mine is no doubt a product of this ragged but persistent femininity.

"Authentic" is a tired word, but I can't think of another one to describe how true femme fits on me. There is little I am more certain about. My femme identity is a product of my past and an iteration of my politics, and also it is an embodiment. Today, I prioritize acrylic nails and false eyelashes above other luxuries in the budget. At the Vietnamese nail salon, I sit by other tattooed women with crooked teeth and tight clothes. We smile and chit-chat with our technicians and each other. It's relaxing there, to be among the sound of the electric drills, the soap operas on the mounted TV, the mix of loud-mouthed English and quiet Vietnamese. Like the insects from home, the nail dryer glows florescent. And my eyelashes! Sometimes people say, "They look so real!" No, they don't, I think, and I like it that way. They look like a drag queen, they look cheap, they look exactly how I feel. Queer and over-the-top and batting my eyes like Ammie would on a red carpet.

My gender is as rooted in my class as it is my sexuality. It is apparent in my desires—my love of queer masculinity, especially the butches who look like they could fix a car. "The working-class and ethnic roots of the femme-butch couple create a more immediately gratifying experience; it is a stylish, vibrant image that reflects the flamboyance of survival, the heat of lesbian erotic desire, and our loud demand for respect," says Jewelle Gomez. And it is apparent in my friendships—my "femmeships," we say—with other queer femmes. Here too: especially the ones who look like they could fix a car, but in heels.

Sometimes people ask if I knew I was queer before moving to Chicago. People like a "born this way" story when it comes to queer desire. The answer is, not really. But femme? Yes, femme has felt like a quiet whisper in my ear for as long as I can remember. In some ways, given the women of my early life and the land I knew them on, it is impossible that I would be anything but.

PART 5

FAREWELL
TRANSMISSION

"The real truth about it is, no one gets it right."
—Songs: Ohia

31.
We Will Be Gone but Not Forever

I haven't lived in Ohio since 2003. That's seventeen years ago. A full teenage life has come and gone. I go back—go 'home', I still say—at least twice a year, preferably three times, to see Mom, Uncle Dana, Nana, the smokestacks. I have lived as long elsewhere as I have there. I have fallen in love and been broken in Chicago, Minneapolis, Boston. I got a PhD, I became firmly queer, I have crawled my way above the poverty line and then back under it (and then back up again) in other midwestern cities and that one time on the East Coast. But home, Home, *home* has always been Cleveland. Even when it hasn't been.

In 2010, a bit over a year into the recession, Mom will lose her job at the print shop at the lighting factory. She will break the news in apologetic hysterical sobs in a hotel room we share for Kat's wedding. My partner at the time, Mike, will squeeze my shoulders and remind me that this is why we fight capitalism. Mom will not find a "good" job ever again, and she will be thrown into poverty and trailer parks and depression all over again. I will be hundreds and hundreds of miles from her for all of this, and it will break my heart.

With the exception of Nana, all of my grandparents will die while I'm in either Minneapolis or Boston. I will grieve over the phone when Mom shares each death, I will see Ammie in a rainbow when she passes, I will cry on the flights home to the funerals.

I will fall in love so many times. I will be in bands in Chicago, I will be fucked by many men and also women. I will be wooed by anarchist theory, I will be mentored by a Marxist, I will occupy buildings and Michigan Avenue in protest, I will be near-arrested on more than one occasion in acts of collective defiance against the State. I will trust the value of these actions in my bones.

I will believe I have met a man who is worth stifling my queerness. A man worth some version of marriage that doesn't make my stomach turn. The best man you will ever meet. A communist and a true partner. And handsome, so handsome. I will love him bigger than any man before him. He will have the same name as my father. He will be so kind, so steadfast. I will leave him. ("In the end I became allergic to security," writes director Silas Howard, another poor-raised queer.)

I have lived so many lives through love.

On the morning of my thirtieth birthday, I will have a dream. It is of Ron in my doorway, and the diary, and the weight of his body. But in this dream, my mother is in the corner on a bench, watching this all unfold. And she is doing nothing.

Later that day, I will have a breakdown on a frozen street in Montreal. I will scream at my partner that he will never understand what it is like to be me. I will push and nearly choke him. I will collapse on the ice. I will shake, and later I will not remember the details of any of this.

I will be diagnosed with C-PTSD. I will confront my mother. I will let myself be angry. And then I will heal, or at least be in the process of it. Mom will get worse before she gets better, but then she will get an apartment in Lakewood on the water, overlooking the skyline of Cleveland that I will likely someday get tattooed on my body. She will take medicine that makes her brain less burdened, and I will be so glad. She will get a job driving rental cars to and from the airport. I will continue to love her and love her and love her more than anything. I will continue to say "Goodnight, Momma!" no matter what time of day.

And when I visit home (home-home), when I stay in my uncle's attic and share wine with him, and walk to Phoenix coffee shop on Coventry, and see movies at the Cedar Lee, I will remember.

I will visit my father in a nursing home with wallpaper and carpet and dense air. Frances has died, so now that she's out of the way, Mom comes with me. Daddy recognizes me every time. He recognizes Mom too. But he doesn't remember anything else. I remind him who my partner is, I remind him where I live, what I do. I try to sit with him and share stories I've heard before—about how he stapled my shorts (with me in them) to the roof of the shed so he could install shingles and so I wouldn't fall off, about our dog Caesar, about watching him on the racetrack, about the one time he gave me sips of his beer at a St. Patrick's Day party and how, between that and the shamrock cookies I ate, Mom spent the rest of the night cleaning up green puke. He will nod, laugh sometimes. He will say, "Oh yeah?" a lot, as though he's so interested to learn about the things he used to do before the accident, before he was so bored.

"There's nothin' to do here," he will say, and he is right. I will hug him goodbye and say, I love you, and he will usually not say it back. I will research places for people with brain injuries in Ohio and find out that unless you are a war vet, there is nothing for you. I will make lists of things that might make him less miserable. His hands are too shaky for model cars now, his brain too tired even for TV. Sometimes after a visit, Mom will need a moment by herself. *This was her husband.*

Often, I will meet friends in Ohio City, and I will pass the Guardians of Traffic. I will wonder if they are appropriative, in their emulation of Native aesthetic. I learn that the sculptor who constructed them in 1932 is Henry Hering and that his wife, Elsie Ward, quit her own career as a sculptor to support her husband's work. I will like them less after learning this.

Often, when I come home, I will gaze at the smokestacks. Look . . .

32.
Fe_2O_3

Any iron matter, over time, in combination with too much oxygen and water, will corrode into rust. Bioluminescence—what allows the lightning bug to glow, even after its death—it too requires oxygen. Just like rust. Just like us.

Sometimes by the end of the day, the lipstick I smear daily across the edges of my mouth will chip and flake. Amidst the deep red stain, the lines of my lips will emerge as if palms being read for fortune; revealing like a map, a topography of my thirst, my hunger, my breath. And in my unkemptness, in the cracked parched brokenness, in the deep copper tawny hue of it, I am reminded of home.

I breathe easier when I am in Ohio. My lungs grow bigger there. I am surrounded by decay, graffiti that begs the governor for a clean needle exchange . . . I am sometimes on the same street that took my father. And yet.

There is something to be said for ruins beyond the exotification of them. They are not romantic, nor are they only evidence of capitalism's inevitable outcomes, but rather they are, paradoxically, some semblance of resilience. Some evidence of how we go on anyway. How, otherwise, we are fine.

I grew up with rust, buildings abandoned and crumbling like steady snow, but these women I loved, this femme I became, we survived it. We survive it. We do our lips anyway.

Rust Belt Femme Mixtape

(chapter references)

Epigraph. "Farewell Transmission," Songs: Ohia

1. "We Are The Champions," Queen
2. The Coven of Persistent Lampyridae
3. "Sunshine On My Shoulders," John Denver
4. "Otherwise, I am fine "
5. "Bad Reputation," Joan Jett
6. "People," Barbra Streisand
7. A Memory before the Accident
8. "Creep," Radiohead
9. "Outro with Bees," Neko Case
10. "All I Really Want," Alanis Morisette
11. "Come as You Are," Nirvana
12. "Fuck and Run," Liz Phair
13. "So Much for the Afterglow," Everclear
14. […]
15. Momma
16. "That Day," Poe
17. "Open heart furnaces light up the sky"
18. 1999
19. Ammie
20. 2001
21. "... a city to cover with lines ..."
22. "Artificial Light," Rainer Maria
23. "Closed Hands," Saetia
24. "Confessions of a Futon Revolutionist," The Weakerthans
25. "For Me This Is Heaven," Jimmy Eat World
26. "Alien She," Bikini Kill
27. "Spectacular Views," Rilo Kiley
28. *The Hum of the Electric Air!* The One AM Radio
29. "Ooh Do I Love You," Cap'n Jazz
30. "Jason's Basement," Gossip
31. "Farewell Transmission" Kevin Morby and Waxahatchee (cover)

Referenced and Recommended Reading

Persistence: All Ways Butch and Femme, eds. Zena Sharman and Ivan Coyote

Undoing Gender, Judith Butler

What You Are Getting Wrong About Appalachia, Elizabeth Catte

Ghostly Matters: Haunting and the Sociological Imagination, Avery F. Gordon

Rednecks, Queers, and Country Music, Nadine Hubbs

Trash: Short Stories, Dorothy Allison

Until We Reckon: Violence, Mass Incarceration, and a Road to Repair, Danielle Sered

Mariame Kaba (all of her writing/speaking)

It Was Like a Fever: Storytelling in Protests and Politics, Francesca Polletta

TAZ: The Temporary Autonomous Zone, Ontological Anarchy, Poetic Terrorism, Hakim Bey

"The Future of the Commons," David Harvey

Out in the Country: Youth, Media, and Queer Visibility in Rural America, Mary L. Gray

A Field Guide to Getting Lost, Rebecca Solnit

Queerly Classed, ed. Susan Raffo

"Capitalism and Gay Identity," John D'Emilio

Not Quite White: White Trash and the Boundaries of Whiteness, Matt Wray

"Butchy Femme," Mykel Johnson (in *The Persistent Desire*, Ed. Joan Nestle)

"Identity Politics and Class Struggle," Robin D.G. Kelley

Acknowledgments

Anne Trubek and Martha Bayne are my editors and my heroes. Anne, you took a chance on my proposal with an enthusiasm that gave me courage. Your edits were encouraging and constructive, and you have continued to serve as a model of humor, strength, and bravado. Martha, your edits shaped the details of this book in a way that made it so much stronger than it started. You two are an inspiration to me in how to live a full life with purpose and integrity. Thank you, both.

To the rest of the Belt Publishing family: thank you. David Wilson, you gave me a cover that belongs on a mixtape from 1999, which is to say, it's perfect. Michelle Blankenship, I was so glad to meet you in your studded black dress and bangs, overcome with gratitude that my publicist was also an Ohian with good fashion. Thank you for helping get the word out. And to my fellow Belt Pub authors: I am deeply humbled to be in your company. I am especially grateful that professional affiliation has also enabled friendship—looking at you, Phil Christman (and Ashley Lucas), Rayshauna Gray, Vivian Gibson, Ryan Schuessler, and Kevin Whiteneir Jr. And to the behind-the-scenes folks who make this all possible: Bill Rickman, Meredith Pangrace, Dan Crissman, and Michael Jauchen—thank you!

I am grateful for the community of writers and mentors I have had in my life, past and present, who have helped me hone this craft: Ian Lashbrook, Nadjya von Ebers, Daniel Makagon, Matt Didier, Steve Almond, Timothy Oleksiak (my dear luff), and many more. Thank you also to Jason Albus for the cover photo and the friendship. And deep gratitude to everyone who offered to read early drafts, and to all the stunning writers who provided blurbs—what an honor it was to have your eyes on these early pages.

To everyone named in this book, the Ohio family/chosen-family who shaped me and loved me and gave me something to write about. This book, of course, is nothing without you. To my dear CHS community, Jackie, Colleen, Meg, Gwenny, Teen, and Pan: thank you for your friendship. Kimmy Kat: you are my heart and my sister-of-choice; I love you and your babies forever. Sheri, I hope you see how this is in part an overdue love letter to you; thank you for our memories. To the Lakewood punks and Cleveland FNB crew: thank you. To my early life working-class kids with dirty feet and wild imaginations—you're the core of me. To cousin Jenny: your commitment to keeping us connected has meant more than I can possibly express. I love you, and I thank you. And Meghan W.: what a joyful surprise it's been to feel so connected to you.

To my Chicago people who continue to uplift me wherever we are, and to the community I found in Minneapolis and Boston, I am so grateful. Thanks especially to Michael Silver for being my friend, cheerleader, and family. To Giuseppe for being my forever-hero and teacher. To Jacoby, who is a part of me. And love and thanks to Kristen and Emily D. for our continued connection; to Mish Zimdars, whose solidarity has been unwavering; my CPY family; to Fred for your support; to Louie, Lia, and Vanessa for sharing such nourishing friendship; to Breck for always being there; and to Brad and Katie for all the support, laughs, and love. To Cristela Guerra and Patrick Garvin—you are both treasures; thank you for being. Gabriel Joffe, I appreciate you—and everything you bring to friendships and the world—so very much. To Joe and Alex, thank you for the realizations. Thank you also to Debra Michals and Gordene McKenzie for your encouragement, support, and for being models of the kind of magical woman I want to become. And I owe deep gratitude to Vince Brown, who has been such a beacon of support and encouragement. I have learned so much from you, and I have felt such joy in our friendship. Thank you.

To Crisipin: my first queer romance, my punk Lefty comrade, my bandmate, my Bear, my friend to the end—I love you. To Alana: you are written in my body, and I wouldn't have it any other way; I love you and am so grateful for your influence on my life, my ink, and my music taste. Love and thanks also to: Brian, Jon, Johnny, Neal, Matt, Chuck, and Mike.

Emily Jane Powers, Muffy Davis, Binyamina Barrios: it is rare to find people with whom you can be 100% yourself. Thank you for your empathy, your embrace of nuance, your love. You don't know one another, but the three of you, in similar ways, inspire me to live deeply and authentically and in alignment with my gut. What a gift I have found in each of our respective friendships.

To Meagan: I adore who you are and love our friendship. I have felt so grateful to have you along with me on this book journey, and thank you for your eyes on an early draft, and for the helpful feedback and tips you offered me. I love you, George, and Rosie so very much.

Mark Phinney, what can I say? You have given me so much trust in myself and this dream. You have given me laughing-so-hard-I-can-barely-breathe emotional support, snacks when I'm hangry, and help with my car. You are my friend to the end. I love you so much and am thankful for you so much. Thanks also to the whole Sbux family.

To my queerworld: Angela, Karisa, Eli, Elizabeth, EG, Libby, and our dear, late Jesús—you're here in these pages too. Same goes for you Dana S., my dear, supportive friend: thank you for who you are. Love also to Kaitlyn, Matt, Marla, Liora, Diane, Jason Q., Molly W., Steph R., and many more. And Melody: my sister Aquarius killjoy—who would I be without you? (I don't even want to think about it!)

To my fellow working-class femmes: Shannon Weber, my sister and heart, I love you; Angela Carter, you have helped me find language for our being, and I'm lucky for you; Krystal,

Erica S., Jaime K., and all my other internet working-class femme sisters: this is for you, for us.

To the witches that moved this along: To the Moon Babes Collective, Angela T, Claire, grey, Lacey and the Future, Amy K., Bri, and others, I am so grateful for your magic. To Rae McCarthy, I made the best decision to hire you as my feminist life coach at the very beginning of this process—thank you for your guidance.

Momma: no love will ever be as big as the one we share together. You have given me everything. I love you more than any book could express. Thank you, truly, for everything. And to the rest of our family who are also at the heart of this book—Chris, Uncle Dana, Ammie and Daddad, Gramps and Nana, the Wettas and the Jacksons, the Neuzils, and the Krausses— thank you for your love and support.

Logan: you are my best friend and my person. None of this would be possible without you. You have been so generous with your time, your resources, and your love. Thank you for your edits. Thank you for being there through the highs and the lows. Thank you for seeing me. I see you too. More life, together, please. I love you.